THE RUSSIAN EMPIRE

1855-1914

A-R. Faces of the 1860's.

A.

B.

C.

D.

E.

F.

G.

H.

I.

J.

K.

L.

M.

N.

O.

P.

Q.

R.

THE RUSSIAN EMPIRE

A Portrait in Photographs

CHLOE OBOLENSKY

WITH AN INTRODUCTION BY MAX HAYWARD

JONATHAN CAPE THIRTY BEDFORD SQUARE LONDON

First published in Great Britain 1980
Copyright © 1979 by Chloe Obolensky and the Estate of the
late Max Hayward
Jonathan Cape Ltd, 30 Bedford Square, London WC1

British Library Cataloguing in Publication Data
The Russian Empire.
1. Russia—Social life and customs
I. Obolensky, Chloe
947.08'022'2   DK189.2
ISBN 0-224-01796-9

Printed in the United States of America
Originally published in the United States by
Random House, Inc., New York

FOR SERGEI

ACKNOWLEDGMENTS

In the task of locating and assembling the photographs I have received help from many persons and institutions. To list them all would be impossible. I wish, however, to single out and especially thank the following:

Mr. R. Blais, president of the French Geographical Society

Miss Christina Cleve, assistant curator of The Archives for Prints and Photographs, National Museum of Finland

The Clich Laboratory, Paris, France

Dr. A. Duchâteau, director of the Ethnographic Museum of Vienna, Austria

Miss Valerie Lloyd, curator of the Royal Photographic Society of Great Britain

Mr. Bjorn Ochsner, director of the Department for Prints and Photographs, Royal Library, Copenhagen, Denmark

Miss Elizabeth Tokoi, librarian of the Slavonic Department, University of Helsinki, Finland

Dr. Rudiger Vossen, director of the Hamburg Museum of Ethnography

Furthermore, photographs from private collections were generously loaned by:

Mrs. Tania Alexander
Mrs. Serge Andolenko
Count and Countess Vladimir Apraxin
Miss Felicity Ashbee
Mr. L. O. Bek Soffiev
Mrs. Valerian Bibikov
Father Boris Bobrinsky
Mrs. Brujak
Mr. Richard Burton
Professor George Candilis
Princess Olga Cantacuzene
Miss Mary Chamot
Mrs. J. Chatenay
Mrs. Paul Demidoff
Countess Alix Depret Bixio
Princess Olga Djordjadzé
Mr. Rostislav Doboujinsky
Father George Drobot
Baron Patrick de Gmeline
Dr. A. Golovin
Baron Gaston de Grotthuss
The late Mrs. Hitrovo
Miss N. N. Ivanov Lutzevine
Mrs. Alexander Jedrinsky
Mrs. A. Kalinine
Countess A. Kapniste

Mrs. Vladimir Khlebnikov
Count and Countess Kleinmichel
Mrs. Cyril Kniazeff
Mr. Nicholas Komstadius
Mr. and Mrs. Alexander Lodijensky
Mr. and Mrs. Michael Lopoukhine
Mrs. Alexander Lwoff
Mrs. Donald Malcom
Mr. and Mrs. S. Mamontov
Mrs. H. Mazet
Count George Mengden
Marquise Anna de Merindol
Princess Olga Mescherinov
Mrs. M. Miasnovo
Mr. Alexis Miatleff
H.R.H. Prince Michael of Greece
The late Mrs. Helen Tolstoy Miloslavsky
Prince Achille Murat
Mr. and Mrs. B. Nechaieff
Miss Elizabeth Nekludoff
Countess Michael Nieroth
Princess N. S. Obolensky
Princess Nathalie Obolensky
Father Nicholas Obolensky
Prince Nicholas Obolensky
Mrs. Offrossimov

Dr. Nils Oleinikov
Miss Vera Pilkin
Countess V. Mussin Pushkin
Mr. Adam Ridley
Mrs. N. Rodzianko
Princess Vladimir Schakhovskoy
Mrs. Sophie Shatilov
Countess Nicholas Sheremetev
Mrs. Nadia Shidlovsky
Mrs. Lydia Pasternak Slater
Mrs. Serge Solloghub
Mr. and Mrs. Arkady Stolypin
Dr. Szyszman
Countess D. Tatischev
Count Mathew Tolstoy
Mr. and Mrs. François Toutée
Princess Alexander Trubetskoy
Princess Sophie E. Trubetskoy
Mr. B. P. Vakhruschev
Mr. and Mrs. Constantine Veriguine
Mr. and Mrs. Vladimir Volkov
Count Simeon Vorontzoff
Mr. and Mrs. Simeon Vorontsov Veliaminov
Mr. and Mrs. Vladimir Yanushevsky
Mrs. Alexandra Zagatsky
Mr. and Mrs. Michael Zveguintsov

Finally, I owe much to the friendship and devotion of Nadia and Maria Grotthuss and Olga Obolensky, who helped me to unearth most of the photographs relating to Russian family life.

S. Cossack musicians, c. 1880's.

PREFACE

$\mathcal{T}$HE RUSSIAN EMPIRE: A PORTRAIT IN PHOTOGRAPHS was born of an experience which seemed at the time quite accidental. Coming across a small collection of photographs of Russian country life at the turn of the century, I was struck by their unusual beauty, and by the faithfulness with which they seemed to illustrate impressions left from a reading of Russian literature. Later, as I began to look for more material these first rapid impressions gained power and focus, encouraging me not only to see if I could evoke, through original photographs, the salient features of a vanished world, but also to relate this material to the body of Russian literature and historical scholarship.

It is immediately obvious that for a pictorial survey of the main aspects of Russian life over a period of more than fifty years to be at all comprehensive, one would have to assemble several volumes ranging over social, political and cultural matters. This portrait of Russia can claim to be no more than an introduction. In choosing the photographs for this book, I was limited not only by problems of space but also by the selective, not to say haphazard, nature of the sources which I was able to consult. These ranged from salvaged family albums to photographic societies, geographical archives and ethnographic collections in a dozen or so European countries (including the Soviet Union) and in the United States. To watch this heterogeneous material slowly form into a picture which, however incomplete, possessed both coherence and truth was a moving and at times even a startling experience. The photographs assembled here, hardly any of which have been published before, are offered in the hope that the reader will share this experience.

In the main, the book has been planned as a journey, its general course plotted in an eastward direction from the two capitals, St. Petersburg and Moscow, across the Volga, the Ural Mountains and Siberia, to the farthest confines of the empire on the Pacific Ocean —and back—through Central Asia, the Caucasus and the Crimea to Russia's western borderlands on the Carpathians and the Baltic Sea. Better perhaps than an arbitrary selection of themes and events of Russian history, this largely topographical approach (with the emphasis laid on the provinces) will, I hope, give a direct impression not only of the empire's extent, but also of the immense variety of landscapes, nationalities and human occupations which existed within its borders.

I would like to thank the many friends who so generously helped me during the preparation of this book. More particularly, I wish to thank Dimitri Obolensky, who provided knowledge and guidance at different and often crucial stages; Belinda Cadbury for her support and practical assistance; and Lila de Nobili for many perceptive suggestions. To my husband, for his constant help and understanding, my debt is great.

In concluding these introductory words, I feel much sadness at the thought that Max Hayward, to whose inspiration, knowledge and friendship this book owes so much, did not live to see its appearance.

"Τῶ σ' ἄμοτον κλαίω τεθνηότα, μείλιχον αἰεί."

Chloe Obolensky
London, April 1979

xi

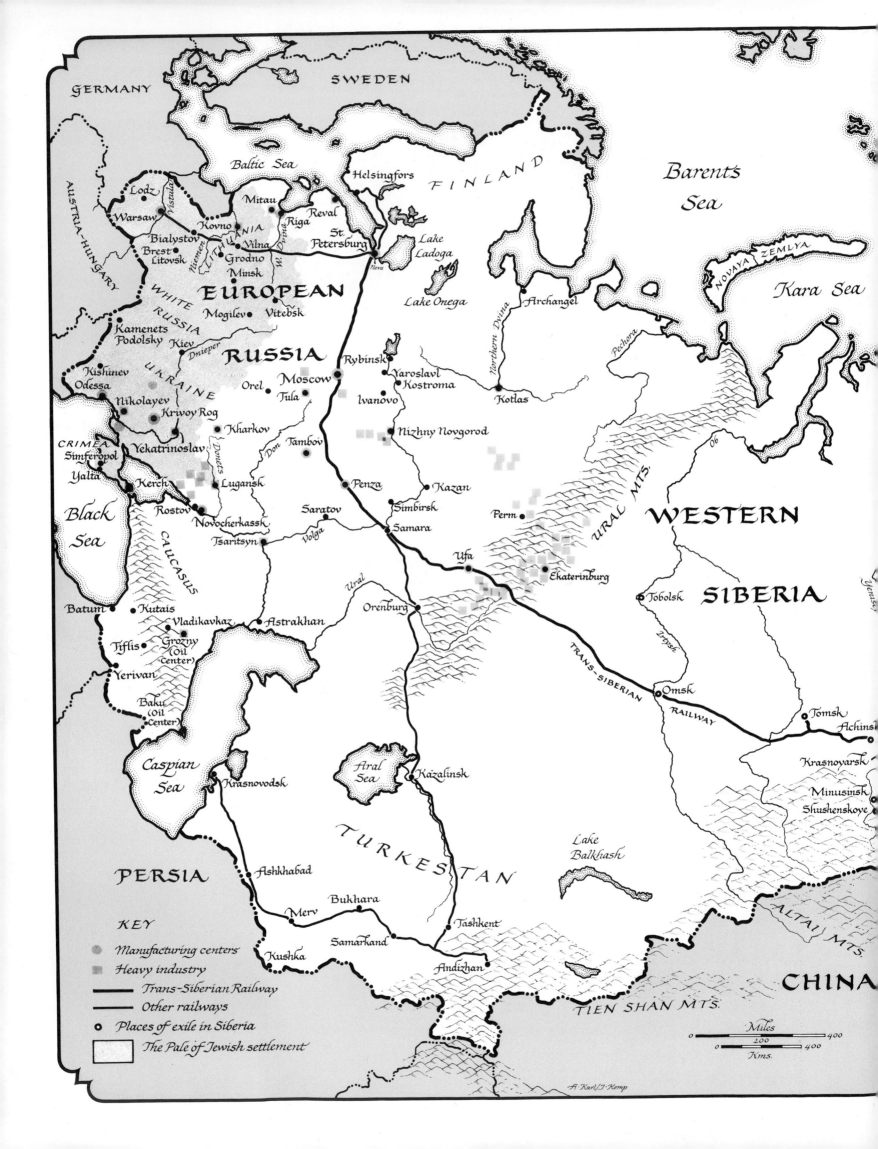

GERMANY

SWEDEN

Baltic Sea

Barents Sea

FINLAND

NOVAYA ZEMLYA

Kara Sea

Lodz
Mitau
Warsaw
Reval
Helsingfors
Kovno
Riga
Bialystov
Vilna
St. Petersburg
Lake Ladoga
Brest Litovsk
Grodno
Minsk

AUSTRIA-HUNGARY

LITHUANIA

WHITE RUSSIA

EUROPEAN

Mogilev
Vitebsk

Lake Onega

Archangel

Kamenets Podolsky
Kiev
Dnieper

RUSSIA

Rybinsk
Yaroslavl
Kostroma

Northern Dvina

UKRAINE

Kishinev
Odessa
Orel
Moscow
Tula
Ivanovo

Nizhny Novgorod

Kotlas

Pechora

Nikolayev
Krivoy Rog
Kharkov

Tambov

Ob

CRIMEA
Simferopol
Yekatrinoslav
Don

Donets
Lugansk
Penza
Kazan

URAL MTS.

WESTERN

Yalta
Kerch

Simbirsk
Perm

Black Sea

Rostov
Novocherkassk
Saratov
Samara

CAUCASUS

Tsaritsyn
Volga
Ufa
Ekaterinburg

SIBERIA

Tobolsk

Batum
Kutais
Vladikavkaz
Astrakhan

Ural
Orenburg

Irtysh

Tiflis
Grozny (Oil Center)

Yenisey

Yerivan

TRANS-SIBERIAN

Baku (Oil Center)

RAILWAY

Omsk

Caspian Sea
Krasnovodsk

Aral Sea
Kazalinsk

Tomsk
Achinsk

Krasnoyarsk

Minusinsk
Shushenskoye

Lake Balkhash

PERSIA
Ashkhabad

TURKESTAN

ALTAI MTS.

Merv
Bukhara

KEY

Kushka
Samarkand
Tashkent

Andizhan

CHINA

TIEN SHAN MTS.

● Manufacturing centers

■ Heavy industry

—— Trans-Siberian Railway

—— Other railways

◦ Places of exile in Siberia

▭ The Pale of Jewish settlement

Miles
0   200   400

0   200   400
Kms.

A. Karl / J. Kemp

Arctic Ocean

N

THE RUSSIAN EMPIRE 1900~1914

Bering Sea

Kolyma

Lower Tunguska

Lena

EASTERN

Viluisk ○   Yakutsk ○

SIBERIA

KAMCHATKA

Sea of Okhotsk

Angara

Amur

SAKHALIN

Lake Baikal

Cheremkhovo ●

Irkutsk ●   Chita ●   ● Nerchinsky Zarod   Khabarovsk ●

Kyakhta ○

MONGOLIA   MANCHURIA

Harbin ●

CHINA

Vladivostok ●

Sea of Japan

JAPAN

NATIONAL AND ETHNIC GROUPS
IN EUROPEAN RUSSIA

55 million ~ Russians	5 million ~ Jews
22 million ~ Ukrainians	4 million ~ Balts
8 million ~ Poles	3 million ~ Caucasians
6 million ~ White Russians	2 million ~ Germans

CHRONOLOGY

1853–1856	Crimean War.
1855–1881	Reign of Alexander II.
1855	Fall of Sevastopol.
1856	Congress of Paris.
1857–1867	Herzen publishes *The Bell* in London.
1857	Moderate protection tariff.
1858–1860	Acquisition of Amur and maritime provinces from China.
1858	Dostoyevsky returns from exile.
1859	Surrender of Shamyl; conquest of Caucasus completed by 1864.
1860–1873	First railway boom.
1860	Founding of Vladivostok; Treaty of Peking.
	Introduction of rural courts.
1861	Emancipation of serfs.
1861	*Italy becomes a kingdom; death of Cavour.*
1861–1865	*Civil War in the United States of America.*
1861	Peasant risings in the provinces.
	Student disorders in St. Petersburg, Moscow and other towns.
1862–1864	Secret revolutionary society called Land and Freedom *(Zemlya i Volya)* first founded.
1862	Financial reform.
	Turgenev (1818–1883) publishes *Fathers and Sons.*
1863	Educational reform.
	Polish rebellion.
1863	*United States Emancipation Proclamation.*
1864	Introduction of *zemstvos.*
1864–1869	Tolstoy (1828–1910) works on *War and Peace.*
1864–1885	Conquest of Central Asia (capture of Tashkent, 1865; capture of Samarkand, 1868; conquest of Khiva, 1873; annexation of Kokand, 1876; capture of Merv, 1884).
1865	D.I.Mendeleyev becomes professor at the University of St. Petersburg.
	Press censorship reforms.

1865	*Assassination of Abraham Lincoln.*
1866	Attempted assassination of Alexander II by Karakozov.
	Dostoyevsky publishes *Crime and Punishment.*
	The Contemporary (Sovremennik) and *Russian Word (Russkoye Slovo)* closed.
1867	Reduction of protective tariffs.
	Sale of Alaska and of the Aleutian Islands to the United States.
	Creation of governor generalship in Turkestan.
1869	*Karl Marx's* Das Kapital *(Vol. I) published.*
	Opening of Suez Canal.
1870	*Outbreak of Franco-Prussian War; German victory at Sedan.*
1870	Abrogation of Black Sea clauses of the Treaty of Paris.
	Municipalities reform; municipal self-government along *zemstvo* lines.
	Abramtsevo acquired by S.I. Mamontov and by 1880 became an influential artists' colony.
	Lenin born.
1871	*German Empire proclaimed (Bismarck becomes Chancellor).*
	Uprisings in Paris; la Commune.
1872	Three Emperors' League (Germany, Austria, Russia).
1873–1877	Depression and industrial crisis.
1874	Military reform; introduction of universal, compulsory military service.
	First "going to the people" movement by the populists *(Narodniki).*
	Moussorgsky's opera *Boris Godunov* first produced (Rimsky-Korsakov's new version made in 1896).
1875	Moslem Tatars revolt: Gaspirali Bey, mayor of Bakhchi Sarai, campaigns in the Volga area with Kazan as center.

1875–1876	Southern Sakhalin ceded to Japan; western Kurile Islands acquired.	1896	Treaty with China: concession for Chinese-Eastern railway.
1876	Organization of the populist society Land and Freedom.	1896–1897	Strike movement.
	First public demonstration in St. Petersburg.		Armenian massacres.
	Bakunin dies in Bern.	1896	Popov gives demonstration of wireless telegraphy.
1877	Tchaikovsky's opera *Eugene Onegin* first produced.	1897	Monetary reforms under Witte; adoption of the gold standard.
	Reintroduction of protective tariffs.		Moscow Art Theater founded by Stanislavsky and Nemirovich-Danchenko.
	Russo-Turkish War.		
1878	Treaty of San Stefano.	1898	Publication of the first issue of *World of Art.*
	Congress of Berlin.		Social Democratic party founded.
	Strikes in St. Petersburg.		Port Arthur leased to Japan.
1878–1881	*Second British war against Afghanistan.*	*1898*	*Spanish-American War.*
1878–1881	Vera Zasulich attempts assassination of General Trepov and is acquitted.	*1899*	The Hague Peace Conference.
			Finnish legislature abolished.
1878–1884	Populist movement.	*1899–1902*	*Boer War.*
1880	General Count Loris-Melikov given extensive powers.	*1900*	*Boxer Rebellion;* Russian occupation of Manchuria.
1881	Assassination of Alexander II.	1901	Russo-Persian Treaty.
1881–1894	Reign of Alexander III.	*1902*	*Anglo-Japanese Alliance.*
1881	Manifesto on *Autocracy;* rise of Pobedonostsev to power.	1903	Menshevist-Bolshevist split in Social Democratic party.
	Beginning of industrial exploitation of the Krivoy-Rog mines.		Abolition of joint-tax liability of peasants.
			Pogroms in Kishinev-Gomel.
	Reduction of peasant "redemption" payments.		Blok publishes his first book of poems.
1882	Creation of the Peasant Agricultural Bank.	1904	Anglo-French Entente Cordiale.
1882–1890	Social legislation (child-labor working hours, factory inspection)	1904–1905	Russo-Japanese War.
1882	Press censorship reinforced.	1905	Fall of Port Arthur; naval battle of Tsushima.
1883	*Triple Alliance (Germany, Austria, Italy) formed.*		Revolution; October Manifesto; Moscow Rising.
	United States Civil Service Act.		V.E. Meyerhold directs theater-studio in Moscow.
1885	Industry picks up.		
1886	Chekhov's first volume of stories published.		Gumilev's first book of poems published.
1887	Reinsurance Treaty with Germany.	1906	Opening of the first Duma.
1889	Introduction of chiefs of district *(Zemskiye Nacholniki).*		Stolypin becomes prime minister; agrarian reform.
1890	*Bismarck resigns.*	1907	Second Duma.
1890	Anti-Jewish legislation enforced.		Second Hague Peace Conference.
1891	Beginning of the Trans-Siberian railroad.		Anglo-Russian Entente.
1891–1892	Famine.		Russo-Japanese Convention.
1892	Witte becomes Minister of Communications, Finance and Commerce.	1907–1912	Third Duma.
		1909	Diaghilev brings the Ballets Russes to Paris.
	Municipal counterreform.	1910	Russo-Japanese treaty.
1893	Industrial boom.		Death of Tolstoy.
	State monopoly on alcohol.	1911	Assassination of Stolypin.
1894	Death of Alexander III.	*1911*	*Turco-Italian War.*
1894–1917	Reign of Nicholas II.		*Outbreak of Balkan wars.*
1894–1895	*Sino-Japanese War.*	1912–1917	Fourth Duma.
1895	Gorky published for the first time.	1912	Anna Akhmatova's first book of poems published.

	Beginning of Mayakovsky's career as a poet.	1914	Russian defeat at Tannenberg.
1913	Mandelstam's first book of poems published.	1915	Russian defeat in Galicia.
	Publication of the Futurist manifesto, *A Slap in the Face of Public Taste*.	1916	Brusilov offensive. Assassination of Rasputin.
1914	*Assassination of Archduke Francis Ferdinand at Sarajevo.*	1917	February Revolution; abdication of Nicholas II; provisional government. October Revolution.
1914–1918	First World War.		

CONTENTS

THE
RUSSIAN
EMPIRE

1855 - 1914

T. Peasants of Nizhny-Novgorod, c. 1880. The women are dressed in the richly embroidered regional costume.

INTRODUCTION

A WESTERN TRAVELER journeying through Russia, Baedecker in hand, at any time in the few decades before the Revolution would probably have come back with visual impressions similar to those that may be gained by scanning the photographs in this volume. They were taken between about 1855 and 1914—years when the Russian Empire was caught up in the many changes that brought it into the "modern world," and ushered in its doom. The photographs indeed constitute a retrospective tour of the old Russia, covering a route that could well have been followed by an enterprising traveler toward the end of the last century or in the early years of this one. After the two capitals, St. Petersburg and Moscow, we see something of the countryside and small towns of the central areas, then cross the Ural Mountains to Siberia, eventually reaching the Pacific Ocean—a journey of six thousand miles which would have been almost impossible for an actual tourist until the completion in 1905 of the Trans-Siberian Railroad from Moscow to Vladivostok. From the Far Eastern region abutting on China we return via Central Asia to the Caspian, the Caucasus, the Black Sea and the Crimea, and finally veer northward through the western part of the empire—which included most of Poland—to the Baltic coast and Finland.

It would have been an incurious traveler who would not have wished to arm himself with some preliminary information on the main historical, social and regional features which have always combined to produce on the outsider an impression of a country so unaccountable in its mixture of the familiar and the totally strange that it has often seemed a puzzle, a bundle of contradictions not to be fathomed by the Western mind. For their part, while sometimes sharing—and even encouraging—this view of themselves, the Russians have traditionally been amused by such lack of comprehension and the corresponding tendency to invent quaint myths about them. There is a well-known, though perhaps apocryphal, Russian story about a French traveler in the last century who, on returning to Paris, wrote a book in which he related, among other details, that on one occasion he had sat drinking tea under the shady boughs of a majestic *klyukva* tree. This exotic-sounding word introduced for the sake of local color by the Frenchman refers to the humble cranberry, which grows on small bushes, and is now used in Russian to describe the kind of egregious errors to which foreigners are thought to be prone. The visitor may be excused his "cranberries," and the Russian his amusement at them, but it must

be admitted in all seriousness that there is a good deal even in the external aspect of the country to prompt bewildered questions. How, first of all, did the Russian Empire come to cover such an unimaginably vast stretch of the earth's surface and embrace such an extraordinary variety of different peoples? Why did it have two capitals, and why—as one may fancy at the outset from the contrast between these cities—does it seem to present now a "European" and now an "Asiatic" face? Does Russia belong to the West or to the East, to both or to neither? The last question is one that has frequently exercised the Russians themselves and provoked controversy among them.

In its origins Russia was distinctly "European." Its heartland lies in the area along several great rivers—the Western Dvina, the Dnieper and the Volga—which, between them, link the Baltic coast with the Black Sea and the Caspian. The population was Slav and, apart from minor tribal differences, identical in language and race with other peoples to the west and southwest—the ancestors of today's Poles, Czechs, Slovaks, Croats and Serbs. Vikings trading with Byzantium and the Arab world along the river routes organized the eastern Slavs into some kind of loose political entity, of which Kiev, a trading depot on the Dnieper, became the center.

The Vikings were eventually assimilated by the Slavs, leaving behind only the word "Rus" (later turned into "Rossiya") by which they were known and a few personal names, such as "Olga," "Igor" and "Vladimir," which in these Slavicized forms now conceal their Germanic origin. It was the connection with Byzantium which proved decisive for Russia's future when, toward the end of the tenth century, the Eastern form of Christianity was adopted by the ruler of Kiev. According to a picturesque but perhaps fanciful account in the old Russian chronicles, this step was taken as a matter of free choice, after a comparison had been made between the various alternatives to paganism. Islam was rejected because the faithful are not allowed to drink alcohol. It was supposedly the splendor of the great cathedral of St. Sophia in Constantinople which swayed the Russians in favor of Greek Orthodoxy. In becoming part of Eastern Christendom, Kiev also entered the sphere of the Greek-Byzantine culture that went with it. The Russian language was written in a modified form of the Greek alphabet and developed a capacity to express abstract ideas and form new words after the Greek pattern, as Byzantine works of theology, history and geography were translated into it. By the middle of the eleventh century Kiev—now with its own cathedral of St. Sophia—was a city of some consequence in the eyes of the world, and its ruler became linked by dynastic marriages with Poland, France and other Western countries. The title of the ruler of Kiev was a Scandinavian word related to the English "King" and generally translated as "Prince" or "Duke." There were other Russian towns, such as Chernigov, Smolensk and Novgorod far to the north, which also had their princes, but the one in Kiev was recognized as the senior among them and called "Great Prince" (or, more usually in English, "Grand Duke").

But loyalties among the rulers of the various towns—at first little more than fortified trading posts—and to the Great Prince were fragile, and owing to constant internal strife Kievan Russia was denied the political coherence needed to ward off external enemies. Kiev itself was extremely vulnerable to hostile incursions from the East, and in the middle of the thirteenth century, when it was in any case already in decline, it was sacked by the Tatars (sometimes referred to as "Mongols"—the name of the Tatar Horde's ruling elite). After the conversion to Christianity, this was the second most decisive event in Russian history. The center of gravity of Russian life now shifted from the relatively fertile south to the much more inhospitable northeast, where agriculture was hampered by long winters and poor soil. Its only advantage was the shelter afforded by dense forests. From this precarious fastness, the princes of a number of towns—over which Moscow became predominant by the second half of the fourteenth century, when its ruler assumed the title of "Great Prince"—were gradually able to restore Russia's fortunes during a long period of contention among themselves and of diplomatic dealings and intermittent warfare with the Tatars, who themselves in the course of time became enfeebled through internal disunity. It should be emphasized that during the two and a half centuries or so of her submission to the Tatars Russia was not occupied by them, but only paid tribute. It was the prime duty of the princes to collect it, and they had to make humiliating journeys to the capital of their Tatar overlords on the Volga, but apart from occasional punitive raids, there was little direct interference with Russia's internal affairs, and none with the Church—which indeed flourished at this time, playing a crucial part in preserving and reaffirming a sense of national identity after the shock of conquest. The Russians' allegiance to their Byzantine-Christian culture was thus in no way threatened. A number of Tatar words—such as, significantly, the one for "money"—entered the Russian language, but otherwise Tatar influence was mainly visible only in dress and manners, such as the kaftan, and the habit of prostrating oneself before those in authority. (These things naturally did much to persuade later Western travelers of the basically "Oriental" or "Asiatic" nature of the Russians, as did degrading punishments, such as flogging with the knout, visited on high and low alike.) But the psychological consequences of the "Tatar Yoke" were far-reaching. It resulted in a certain remoteness from the rest of Christendom, so that Muscovy—as the successor to Kievan Russia became generally known to its neighbors—turned in on itself and took on the conservative, ingrown aspect of a beleaguered culture deprived of easy communion with its sources and driven, as a matter of self-preservation, to cling to the outer forms of ritual and observance. The need for flexibility in dealing with the Tatars made

for a kind of behavior in relations with foreigners that came to appear in Western eyes as crafty or insidious in "Eastern" fashion.

Just as serious, perhaps, from Russia's point of view, as the Tatar Yoke—and more enduring—were the conflicts which also began to develop in the thirteenth century with the expanding powers to the West—first with the German Order of the Teutonic Knights and Lithuania, and later with Poland and Sweden. As the new Russian state was gradually consolidated by Moscow during the fifteenth and early sixteenth centuries by a process of absorbing all the other principalities—and of simultaneously loosening the Tatar hold—it was natural that the need for territorial security should come to seem paramount. This could, of course, only be obtained by continually pushing back Russia's frontiers over the immense, largely flat and featureless expanses stretching out to seeming infinity on all sides. One has only to look at the map to see that this was the logic imposed by geography on Russian history. It would be oversimplifying, however, to say that Russia was inevitably driven by this logic to adopt a centralized, autocratic form of rule more in the spirit of its waning Asiatic overlords than in that of the rising powers of the West, with whom the contest for territory, much of it inhabited by Russians, would be fiercer and lengthier than anywhere else. There were certainly other potentialities, inherent from Kievan times, in the development of Russian statehood. This was shown by the example of the principality of Novgorod, which in the twelfth century took on the aspect of an oligarchic city-state, not unlike Florence or Venice, and governed itself in accordance with an elaborate rule of law. But Novgorod was subdued by Moscow in the fifteenth century. Its destruction was completed in the next century by Ivan the Terrible, who ruthlessly subdued his own Muscovite aristocracy (the *boyars*) in a way which established the principle of absolute rule once and for all. This was another crucial turning point in Russian history, radically marking it off from that of the rest of Europe, where in the feudal period a precedent had been set for the rise of social groups or classes able to curb the sovereign's power.

The reign of Ivan the Terrible saw the beginning of Russia's expansion. In the east there was little resistance, since the Tatar Golden Horde had by now broken up into the three separate khanates of Kazan, Astrakhan and the Crimea. The first two were conquered by Ivan in the middle of the sixteenth century, giving Russia control of the whole length of the Volga, down to its delta on the Caspian Sea, and opening the way for a rapid and more or less unimpeded Russian advance across the Urals into Siberia. Shortly afterwards Ivan began the much more difficult confrontation with Poland and Sweden, which finally ended in Russia's favor only in the eighteenth century. Muscovy's emergence as a serious rival to its neighbors was accompanied by a significant change in the ruler's title: Ivan the Terrible had himself crowned not as "Great Prince" but as "Czar." The word "czar" (derived from "Caesar") was used by the Russians and other Orthodox Slav nations as the equivalent of "Basileus," the Byzantine term for "Emperor." Its assumption by the rulers of Muscovy at first sight suggested that they saw themselves as the heirs of Rome and Byzantium—with all that this implied in terms of an eventual claim to dominion over the whole of Christendom. The idea of Moscow as the "Third Rome" ("and a Fourth there shall not be") was indeed formulated by a Russian churchman at the beginning of the sixteenth century and seemed reasonable by the lights of the time: Byzantium had fallen to the Turks in 1453, and Muscovy, by now confident of completing its liberation from the Tatars, could well feel entitled to inherit the imperial mantle as the only remaining defender of Orthodoxy. The Byzantine double-headed eagle was adopted as the Russian emblem of state, and various documents were put about purporting to show that the Russian czar was actually descended from the Roman and Byzantine emperors. Yet it is a matter of dispute as to how far the advancement of this claim meant that successive Russian czars seriously embraced the universalist pretensions of their supposed Byzantine predecessors by way of what we should nowadays call an "ideology." Perhaps not to the extent sometimes maintained in a latter-day search for the roots of "Russian imperialism." In their actual dealings with other nation-states the czars, on the whole, displayed a cautious realism not usually found in persons swayed only by some visionary belief. The beguiling thought that they were natural successors to former ecumenical rulers no doubt constantly lurked in their minds as they proceeded, in the course of the next two centuries, to build the largest empire the world has known, but they are just as likely to have been guided mainly by the pragmatic considerations—and in the later stages also by sheer force of inertia —which had made continuous territorial expansion so irresistible to other nations as well. As with other empires, "ideology" for the most part simply followed the flag.

After a brief period of internal political turmoil ("The Time of Troubles") at the end of the sixteenth and beginning of the seventeenth centuries—during which the Poles succeeded for a short time in putting their own man on the throne of Russia—a new dynasty, the Romanovs, resumed under strong absolutist rule the course charted by Ivan the Terrible and his predecessors. The main external preoccupation was henceforth with the Poles and the Swedes, but Russia's decisive thrust to the West came only in the next century, under Peter the Great, and the seventeenth century was more notable, during the reign of Peter's father, for several internal developments. The most important single event was a schism in the Russian Orthodox Church, which toward the end of the preceding century had established its own patriarchate, thus marking its formal independence from the now subjugated Constantinople. The Russian schism was not provoked by the kind of doctrinal problem that had played an important part in the beginning of the breach between the Eastern and Western churches in the ninth century a few years before Russia's conversion to Christianity, but arose from causes that seemed trivial at first sight. The Patriarch, with the approval of the Czar, had invited Greeks to revise the Russian liturgical books and correct errors which had crept in during centuries of recopying. One such error was the misspelling of the name of Jesus. There were also minor divergencies in ritual— the Russians, for instance, made the sign of the cross with two fingers instead of with three, as in current Byzantine practice. The motive for correcting these faults was to enhance the credentials of Moscow as the new center of Orthodoxy, but such "interference" by the Greeks in the affairs of their Church was bitterly resented by many Russians. It was argued that while Byzantium, for its sins, had fallen to the Turks, Russia had survived and grown strong—which must mean that the faith had been preserved in pristine form. And there was also a suspicion that the Greeks—many of whom had

taken refuge in Italy after the fall of Constantinople—might be trying to smuggle in "Latin heresy" under the guise of the ostensibly formal modifications they proposed. The leader of the opposition was an intransigent priest called Avvakum, who, in his stubborn single-mindedness, was the precursor of many Russian dissenters to come. The example of him and his numerous followers (called "Old Believers") belies the notion that all Russians have always been slavishly submissive to authority. Avvakum was probably the first person of note to be sent to Siberia for his beliefs. He described his experiences in a moving account of his life, which can still be read as a work of literature. The persecution of the Old Believers gave rise in time to the formation of several religious sects which were distinguished by their total rejection of ecclesiastical and secular authority. Some of them were very extreme and bizarre—the one, for example, which practiced self-castration—and they were clearly the product of a profound and lasting disarray provoked by the schism in the Russian religious consciousness.

Another less dramatic but nonetheless significant development during the reign of Peter the Great's father in the later seventeenth century was the beginning of a slow percolation into Russia of Western cultural influences and manners. This was the inevitable effect of contact—albeit antagonistic—with Poland. The smoking of tobacco, though still mentioned in scandalized tones, was one example. More serious was the idea of a secular art and literature. The written word, when not used for official or commercial purposes, had hitherto been the almost exclusive preserve of the Church, but now there were examples of its use in verse and in plays for the theater, a new source of entertainment in a few private houses and also at the Czar's court. The techniques of icon painting began to be applied occasionally to secular portraits. Much of all this was imitative of Polish or other foreign models, but it was the start of what might have been a slow, organic and relatively painless assimilation by Russia of what it wanted or needed from the West. In the upshot, however, this happened in a very different way.

The story of Peter the Great's brutally rapid and abrupt "Europeanization" of Russia at the beginning of the eighteenth century is too familiar to need recounting in any detail. It was as shattering and fateful in its consequences as anything in previous Russian history, and it created traumas and cultural ambiguities which could not easily be absorbed or resolved by following generations. Peter's idea was a simple one, and he carried it out with a ruthless, overbearing energy never perhaps equaled by any other reforming autocrat. It had been borne in on him during his visit as a young man to Holland and England that to continue the expansion of her frontiers Russia would have to borrow all the necessary arts of war and peace from Western Europe. The first priority was the building of a navy to defeat the Swedes and secure Russia's hold on the Baltic—and also on the Black Sea, which was controlled by the residual Tatar domain in the Crimea (now under Ottoman suzerainty). He laid the foundations of Russian heavy industry by creating ordnance factories, manned by conscripted serfs, in the Urals. Knowing it would be precarious in the long run to rely on the borrowed achievements of Western science and technology, he established institutions of higher learning, at first with a practical emphasis on subjects such as navigation, medicine and mathematics. But his grander vision of an Academy of Sciences was realized after his death, and just after the middle of the century the first Russian university was founded in Moscow. Young Russians were sent abroad to study, and foreign teachers were invited to Russia. In a very few years a country that for centuries had been culturally self-contained, admitting outside influence only in very controlled fashion, suddenly began to take on an alarmingly cosmopolitan appearance—at least in Moscow and the new capital of St. Petersburg, where the upper classes adopted Western-style dress and were compelled by imperial fiat to shave off their beards. The Russian language was flooded with barbarous-sounding and ill-digested foreign words, and the resulting jargon was only gradually domesticated and turned into a more or less harmonious amalgam by Russia's first great writers, such as Pushkin, at the beginning of the nineteenth century. As though to symbolize this portentous change in Russia's whole aspect, Peter began to style himself in a manner more immediately recognizable to the West by including the Latin word "Imperator" in his title.

The greatest and most conspicuous outward token of the new Europeanized Russia was, of course, St. Petersburg. The "old" capital of Moscow kept its status for ceremonial occasions, such as the coronation of a new czar, but after some hesitation on the part of Peter's immediate successors, St. Petersburg was henceforth to be the seat of the court, and the administrative center of the vast and still expanding empire. Peter mobilized all necessary men and materials to build the city at great speed—and at a high cost in human life—on land wrested from the Swedes and inhabited by a sparse population of Finnish fishermen. Nothing could have been more unsuitable as the site of a new city than this marshy delta of the Neva River—as would be attested by generations of pallid government clerks, students and other downtrodden inhabitants of the kind so frequently portrayed in nineteenth-century Russian literature. It was intended not only, in the famous phrase, as a "window on Europe," but also as the clear expression of a challenge: "from here we shall threaten the Swedes," in Pushkin's words. The city served notice that henceforth Russia would fight its Western neighbors, if necessary, in the panoply of their own most advanced technical skills. But it took the rest of the century to absorb more than just the cruder externals of what the West had to offer. Andrey Sinyavsky has put it brilliantly: "In the eighteenth century Russia was ruled mainly by women. It was not of course mere chance or the whim of fate that placed almost only representatives of the weaker sex on the autocrat's throne in such a cruel and, on the whole, virile century. A certain design is discernible here—something which allowed the century's profile to assume a softer, blander outline . . . Peter's edifice had to be made habitable and needed all those finishing touches that could best be added by women with their understanding of service at table, cuisine, fashions, and other such domestic matters. Thanks to the rule of these barbarian women with a weakness for entertainments, dresses, masquerades and courtly manners, Russian civilization assimilated Western ways and tastes with such natural ease that a hundred years after Peter it was able to rear a Pushkin in its lively and fragrantly hot-house atmosphere . . . Without women on the throne . . . neither Russian classicism nor Russian baroque could have brought forth their golden fruit on the swamp turned by Peter into a building site."

The "golden fruits of Russian classicism and baroque" (many of them the work of Italian architects, such as Rastrelli) are visible in the photographs of public buildings, palaces and magnificent interiors in St. Petersburg, but it is also evident from contrasting views of Moscow, and of small towns in the provinces—and even of street scenes in St. Petersburg itself—that Peter's "Europeanization" of Russia, so splendidly manifested in architecture, affected only the upper crust of society, becoming progressively less apparent the further it radiated out from the new capital, and the lower one descended in the social scale. Moscow, a homely, sprawling city, often fondly likened by its inhabitants to a large village, inevitably began to pride itself on being the "more Russian" of the two capitals. The difference between them was reflected in a number of everyday ways—in the dress of the bearded Moscow merchants, for example, with their leather boots and double-breasted kaftans (as opposed to the European-attired shopkeepers of St. Petersburg), and even in speech, that of St. Petersburg a little clipped, with members of the upper classes sometimes affecting a French pronunciation of their r's, while Moscow's was pleasantly rounded and drawling, and less prone to the use of foreign words. Yet, though it was often disdainfully described as such even by Russians, Moscow was never "Asiatic" in any meaningful sense. Much in the city's general appearance, as in the case of other older Russian cities, is due to earlier, more archaic influences no less "European" than those which went into the making of St. Petersburg, but assimilated more slowly —and in the process modified over the ages in ways that lend them a peculiarly "Russian" flavor. Moscow's main glory, the Kremlin (the word means "citadel," and other Russian cities also have kremlins), is partly the work of Italian architects who were invited in the fifteenth century—by Ivan the Terrible's grandfather—to reconstruct and add to it, with results that justify a Russian poet's description of it as "Florence in Moscow." The numerous churches that are the most striking feature of any older Russian city—Moscow, with pardonable hyperbole, traditionally claimed to have "forty forties" of them—ultimately derive from a Byzantine model, but transformed to such an extent (notably by the addition of a larger number of cupolas) that they came to be the most familiar distinguishing mark of the Russian scene.

Even more important, perhaps, than the material impact of Western Europe on Russia during the eighteenth century was the borrowing of its artistic forms—in literature, the theater, music, ballet and painting, etc. The first products of this apprenticeship were often imitative and sterile, rarely—at least in literature—rising above a gauche "neoclassicism," but they prepared the way for the uniquely rich and original achievements of the following century. If a millennium of slow, tortuous, constantly menaced cultural development thus at last came to brilliant fruition, it cannot be denied that Peter's precipitate "opening to the West" was mainly responsible. This positive side of what he did makes it difficult, even now, for many Russians to draw up a final balance sheet of his reign. He was cruel and arbitrary in the way he imposed his reforms, trampling on and flouting age-old habits. Forcing his subjects to ape the ways of Europe, he violated Europe's very spirit. Having been impressed, for instance, by the salons in the Western capitals he had visited during his youthful grand tour, he *ordered* the nobility of St. Petersburg to attend social gatherings together with their wives, who had up to now been segregated in almost Oriental fashion. This comic episode was typical of his entire approach. The wholesale importation of the material and cultural benefits of the Renaissance —in which Russia had not partaken—was deliberately carried out in such a way as to make a mockery of the humanism at the basis of them. Instead of blending naturally with the country's own established traditions, all these sudden innovations had a dislocating effect which probably underlies much of what to foreigners seems overwrought about the "Russian soul." They created a feeling of unreality which came to haunt the Europeanized elite—particularly the intellectuals, who, feeling neither entirely "European" nor entirely "Russian," found themselves more and more painfully concerned during the nineteenth century at the enormous cultural gulf between themselves and the ordinary people. The famous controversy between the "Slavophiles" and the "Westernizers" raised the question of Peter's responsibility for this situation, and both sides were agreed that a way must be found to make the nation whole again. Yet the profound disturbance in the national psyche caused by Peter's reforms was perhaps not unfruitful: it certainly contributed to the peculiar moral climate in which the hypersensitive mind of a Gogol or a Dostoyevsky constantly received the kind of impressions that make their work so alive to the dilemmas and paradoxes of human existence in general. Fittingly, the main hero of some of their most significant works is St. Petersburg itself, the epitome of everything that both troubled and nourished their imaginations. The elegant "Northern Palmyra," with its rows of Italianate palaces, its magnificent granite-clad embankments, the bridges over the Neva and finely wrought iron grilles along its canals, seemed like the phantom emanation of some stupendous sorcery. As the seat of the world's most omnipotent officialdom it weighed heavily on its citizens, often inducing black melancholia or persecution mania—a frequent theme in St. Petersburg literature is appropriately that of the split personality, or the "double." The most balanced view of what Peter and his city meant to Russia is given by Pushkin in his poem *The Bronze Horseman* (the title refers to St. Petersburg's most striking monument, the equestrian statue of Peter by the French sculptor Falconet), in which admiration for the Czar's work is tempered by compassion for the victims it would always continue to claim.

By the end of the eighteenth century, thanks particularly to a great deal of building under Catherine the Great, St. Petersburg had more or less assumed its final shape and at the same time the Russian empire reached almost to its final extent—apart, that is, from the conquests made in Central Asia in the second half of the nineteenth century, and the acquisition of several smaller areas. Crushing defeats inflicted on Sweden and Poland in the west, and on the Ottoman-controlled Crimean Tatars in the south—as well as the beginnings of Russian penetration into the Caucasus—led not only to a huge accretion of territory, but also to the incorporation of various whole nations and ethnic groups, some of which contributed importantly to Russian life and culture. The retrieval from Poland, already beginning at the end of the seventeenth century, of extensive regions in the west and southwest populated mainly by Russians had the effect of practically doubling the country's Slav stock. But these were "Russians" with a difference. A consequence of the destruction of Kievan Russia in the thirteenth century and the subsequent occupation of much of its territory, first by the Lithuanians and then by the Poles, was that during the long period

of the formation of a new Russian state centered on Moscow some perceptible divergencies inevitably appeared between the "Great" Russians—as those of Muscovy were called—and the "White" and "Little" Russians in the Polish-dominated lands to the west and southwest. The Great Russians were certainly affected by centuries of intermarriage with non-Slav peoples—hence the broad faces with high cheekbones often thought "typically Russian"—and by the time they had regained all the areas lost after the sack of Kiev in 1240, other pronounced differences in language and general outlook had come to mark them off from the population there, despite common origins in historical times. A vital continuing bond, on the other hand, was that most of the White Russians and Little Russians, despite pressures to convert to Roman Catholicism, had remained Orthodox; but, all the same, their long contact with the Poles had exposed them to Western influences and permeated their speech with Polish words. All this was further emphasized by a contrast in the physical environment. In "Little Russia" (or, as it is now called, the Ukraine—literally, "Borderland") the rather bleak, heavily forested and inclement Russia of the north gradually yields to rich, open steppe land (famous for its "black earth"), which, despite the oceanlike monotony of its horizons and severe winters, has an altogether more "southern" aspect. The image evoked by the Ukraine in the minds of Great Russians is of a land more abundant than their own, and of a people more vivacious, who speak with a pleasing lilt and live in whitewashed, straw-thatched adobe houses— very unlike the gray wooden *izby* of the North—with gardens of sunflowers, watermelons and hollyhocks. In the nineteenth century a great poet, Taras Shevchenko, gave shape to a separate Ukrainian consciousness, which in turn led to a movement for autonomy or independence from the "Muscovites," as the Great Russians, somewhat pejoratively, were often called. The same tendency developed later among the much less numerous White Russians (also known as Byelorussians) who live to the northwest of the Ukrainians in an undulating, wooded landscape with abundant streams, lakes and marshes, with fishing a major occupation. Because of the peculiarities of their speech, as well as the preservation of ancient folk customs, many White Russians began to feel entitled to the distinct identity already conferred by long separation from their coreligionists further east.

Another important result of the reacquisition of these ancient territories was that Russia inherited from her defeated and dismembered rival the largest Jewish community in the world. In the fourteenth century, because of intolerable persecution, there was a large exodus of Jews from Germany to Poland during the reign of a king who encouraged their migration at a time when other settlers with urban skills (including Germans and Scots) were being imported to help populate the towns in his entirely feudal country. Many of the Jews settled in villages or small towns in the eastern part of the country where the landlords were Polish and the local peasantry White Russian or Ukrainian. In some of these places they formed the majority of the population. First under Polish and then under Russian rule—as almost everywhere else in Europe—while due advantage was taken of their services as traders or craftsmen, they were subject to a formidable array of disabilities and restrictions, and the threat of violence always hung over them, particularly when difficult times called for scapegoats.

Nevertheless, in precarious coexistence with their neighbors, the Jews of this region struck such deep roots in the local way of life over five centuries that they seemed inseparable from it: Jewish artisans, innkeepers or musicians (who could well be invited to entertain at a Christian wedding) became a familiar part of the scene—though always standing out from it because of their religion, dress and the use of Yiddish, a medieval German dialect with Hebrew and Slav elements in the vocabulary. Under Russian rule they were confined by law to the areas (the Pale of Settlement) already inhabited by them in Polish times, but there were various loopholes, and during the nineteenth century small Jewish communities with their synagogues arose in St. Petersburg, Moscow and other cities outside the Pale, even in Siberia. A series of pogroms which began toward the end of the nineteenth century—and which were connived at if not fomented by the secret police as the traditional means of canalizing popular discontent in areas heavily populated by Jews—provoked large-scale emigration from the Pale of Settlement to the West, particularly to America. On the other hand, by the twentieth century many Jews outside the Pale had assimilated or adapted to Russian society—not always at the price of abandoning their religion—and were playing an increasingly important part in the country's cultural life (music, the arts, literature and scholarship), as well as in spheres such as commerce and law. (Other small Jewish communities were later incorporated into the Russian Empire: e.g., those of Bokhara in Central Asia and the "Mountain Jews" of the Caucasus—both speaking Iranian languages—and the Tatar-speaking Jewish sect known as the Karaim, who lived mainly in the Crimea.)

The crushing of Poland and Sweden in the eighteenth century also brought into the empire the small but highly prized countries now known as the Baltic States: Estonia, Latvia and Lithuania (the last of which had once independently ruled over White Russia and a large part of the Ukraine, before concluding a union with Poland in the sixteenth century). Their capitals, Tallin, Riga and Vilnius, were medieval cities of a Western kind with narrow streets and fine Gothic and Romanesque architecture. From the early Middle Ages the indigenous peoples of Latvia and Estonia had been under the rule of a German landowning class, many of whose members soon began to distinguish themselves in the service of Russian autocracy, mostly in the higher reaches of the administration, the police and the army. Though they retained their German titles of nobility, these "Baltic barons" often became Russified in the course of time, and were noted for their devotion to duty. In Lithuania there was a native aristocracy which, however, became completely Polonized after the union with Poland—only the peasantry continued to speak Lithuanian, an Indo-European language which is of major interest because of its preservation of features elsewhere extinct. Like the German landowners and the German merchants who dominated the trade in the cities, the Latvian and Estonian peasants—close in language to the Lithuanians and Finns, respectively—were mostly Lutherans, while the Lithuanians had become Catholics as a result of their long association with Poland. (During the Lithuanian-Polish domination over White Russia and the Ukraine there were some attempts to "win back" the local population from Orthodoxy, and some success was achieved at the end of the sixteenth century by the creation of the so-called Uniate Church, which allowed the use

of the Eastern rite in return for allegiance to Rome.)

If the Baltic area, with a social structure and general aspect of an essentially Western European type, formed a rather incongruous appendage to Russia, the same was even more true of Poland. By the three partitions—with Prussia and Austria—at the end of the eighteenth century, Russia obtained all the territory to which she had a legitimate historical claim, but early in the next century she also seized most of Poland proper, including the capital, Warsaw, and the great textile city of Lodz. Until they eventually regained their independence after the First World War, the fervently Catholic Poles remained the most recalcitrant of the subject peoples in the Russian Empire, and as visitors to Warsaw could see at a glance, Poland was the measure by which Russia's distinctiveness from the West could most easily be gauged.

The early nineteenth century also saw the annexation of two further countries at Russia's western extremities: in the north, Finland—which was, however, allowed to retain considerable internal autonomy; and in the south, Bessarabia, whose incorporation brought Russia to the threshold of the Balkans and gave her a Rumanian-speaking population, together with such local minorities as Sephardic Jews (whose language was the slightly Hebraicized Spanish called Ladino), Bulgarians and Gypsies. The latter stirred the imagination of Pushkin, who after a visit to Bessarabia wrote one of his most famous poems about them. By way of Poland and Central Europe other groups of Gypsies also entered Russia, which, with its wide-open spaces and traditional tolerance of vagrants, was naturally congenial to them. They followed the same occupations as elsewhere —tinkering, horse trading, fortune-telling, etc. As musicians and singers in fashionable places of entertainment they came to have a place in the upper-class life of St. Petersburg and Moscow, where romantic marriages between Russian noblemen and Gypsy women were not unknown.

The Russian conquest in the late eighteenth century of the north shore of the Black Sea with its fertile and sparsely settled hinterland (known as New Russia) resulted in the incorporation into the empire of the defeated Crimean Tatars, who had once been part of the Golden Horde and came under Ottoman rule in the late fifteenth century. Many of them preferred to emigrate to Turkey rather than accept Russian domination, but enough remained to count as a substantial part of the Crimea's population—and to achieve renown for the excellent wines they produced—until the end of the Second World War, when they were all deported to Central Asia. As elsewhere in the Ottoman Empire—in whose commerce and administration they played a prominent part—there were many Greeks in the Crimea, and from the end of the eighteenth century they formed the nucleus of a large Greek colony—chiefly merchants, but later also professional people such as doctors and teachers— which gradually extended to all the towns along the Black Sea coast: Mariupol, Taganrog and particularly Odessa, the great port founded by Catherine the Great, in which Greeks and Jews became the most notable elements of a very heterogeneous population. (The Greeks who settled along the Black Sea coast after the Russian defeat of the Crimean Tatars were following in the footsteps of their distant ancestors, who had established colonies in the region in ancient times.)

Of all the areas to fall under Russian control at the end of the eighteenth and the beginning of the nineteenth centuries the most exotic in terms of its physical and human geography was the immense Caucasian mountain range, which stretches over six hundred miles from the northeast corner of the Black Sea to the Caspian. This formidable barrier between Asia and Europe, inhabited by dozens of different peoples speaking difficult and mutually incomprehensible languages, made a deep impression on the Russian imagination, and no other part of the empire occupies such an important place in Russian literature. The heart of the Caucasus, both geographically and culturally, is Georgia, whose last king, at the very beginning of the nineteenth century, voluntarily put his country under Russian suzerainty in order to save it from the Persians. For similar reasons, but at a slightly later date, the Christian Armenians to the south also accepted Russian rule as a lesser evil than conquest by the neighboring Muslim powers. Both Armenia and Georgia—once on the easternmost marches of the Byzantine Empire—had been converted to Christianity some six centuries before the Russians and boasted ancient literatures written in their own distinctive alphabets. With such an irrefutable claim to represent a far older civilization, the Georgians and Armenians are inclined to think of themselves as more advanced than the Russians and often chafed under their rule, but the overwhelming need for the Orthodox Czar's protection gave them little alternative but to acquiesce to it. Until the coming of the Russians, the Christian kingdoms in the Caucasus were extremely vulnerable to Muslim incursions—all the more so in that many of the small tribes in the mountains of the north Caucasus, such as the Circassians, the Chechens and the Lesghians, had at various times been converted to Islam during successive invasions by the Arabs (in the seventh century and later), and then by the Persians and the Turks. The most numerous Muslim people in the Caucasus was the one living in the southeast region now called Azerbaijan. In the nineteenth century its inhabitants were always referred to as "Tatars," and since their language—closely related to Ottoman Turkish—generally served as the lingua franca among the mountain tribes, the name was sometimes confusingly applied to other Muslims as well. The area around Baku, the capital of the "Tatars" on the Caspian was known already to the ancient Persians for the inflammable liquid that gushed from its soil and not surprisingly became the center of a fire-worshipping cult. The Russian oil industry was established there in the late nineteenth century.

Russian contact with the Caucasus was prolonged and intimate because of the presence of large military garrisons needed in the sporadic warfare waged for well over half a century with the mountain tribes who stubbornly and bravely resisted Russian domination. The most outstanding of the Muslim leaders was Shamyl who led a "holy war" against the Russians and was subdued only in 1859. In the eyes of many Russian officers who served there over the years it was a uniquely "romantic" setting and, through them, this view of it became well established in the salons of St. Petersburg. Georgia, with its mountains higher than the Alps, its ancient monasteries and churches, and the rich, well-watered lowlands (where the vineyards, said to be the world's most ancient, produce splendid wines such as Tsinandali) made a particular appeal. The Georgians—a race apart, who speak a distinctive Caucasian language unrelated to Indo-European—are a strikingly handsome

people justly renowned for their expansiveness, hospitality, independence and pride, and generations of educated Russians tended to idealize them as being in certain ways exhilaratingly different from themselves. In the work of the two greatest Russian poets, Pushkin and Lermontov, and of later writers, the Caucasus—and Georgia in particular—came to stand for the kind of freedom of the spirit hardly favored by the crushing hierarchies of their own society as it had developed in response to the needs of autocratic rule. It is rare that an imperial relationship has been reflected in the literature of the dominant power in such a fruitful and creditable manner. The same cannot be said of the later Russian thrust into Central Asia on the other side of the Caspian. This was completed in the second half of the nineteenth century and was a nakedly colonial venture (not unconnected with the need for cotton to supply Russian textile factories) which brought under uncongenial Russian rule a number of mainly Turkic-speaking Muslim peoples, ranging from nomads such as the Kirghiz and Turkmens to the ancient urban communities of Samarkand and Bokhara. In the later part of the nineteenth century there was a good deal of Russian settlement on the land in these areas, and a number of new towns were built in Russian "colonial" style.

This rapid sketch of the growth and ethnic composition of the Russian Empire is necessarily incomplete—it would take pages merely to list all the peoples and tribes scooped up by it during its progress over one-sixth of the earth's land surface, and attention has been focused here mainly on those which had an impact on Russian life in general. But there were many others, some of them represented by photographs in the present volume—hunting peoples of Siberia such as the Samoyeds, the Tungus, the Ostyaks and the Yakuts; the Georgian-speaking Khevsurs of the Caucasus, who had strange pagan customs and wore costumes resembling medieval coats of mail; the Kalmucks, a Buddhist Mongol people, noted for their skill with horses, who emigrated from China in the mid-sixteenth century and occupied the arid, salty lowlands north of the Caspian; the oddly Nordic-looking Ainu of Sakhalin, with their animistic religion centered on the cult of the bear. As though this ethnographic wealth were not enough, numbers of colonists from neighboring countries came to live in Russia at various times: Orthodox Serbs from the Austro-Hungarian and Ottoman empires were invited to occupy lands in "New Russia" after its conquest under Catherine the Great, who also settled Germans on the Volga near Saratov, in the justified belief that they would set an example of good husbandry; in the later nineteenth century many Chinese and Koreans came into the country via the newly acquired Far Eastern regions; there was a Chinese quarter in Vladivostok, and Chinese tea merchants were a familiar sight in Nizhni-Novgorod. But unlike America, Russia was not a "melting pot." By and large, each of the many peoples inhabiting the empire kept to its own territory, and there was little internal migration—except, of course, for such natural wanderers as the Gypsies, and to a limited extent the Jews, Armenians and some others. In the later nineteenth and early twentieth centuries, there was considerable officially encouraged movement of Russian and Ukrainian peasants to Siberia (particularly after the building of the Trans-Siberian railroad), but otherwise relatively few left European Russia for these remote areas except as fur traders, miners (of copper, lead and silver as early as the

U. P.L Lavrov, the leader of the Russian populist movement, photographed while supervising an edition of *V'peryod* (Forward), the paper he first published in 1873 in Zurich, and then from London.

V. Members of the Narodnaya Volya.

W, X. These two photographs show a member of the Narodnaya Volya wearing (on the left) his usual everyday clothes, while on the right he is dressed in a "workman's" outfit. This tactical procedure was often, though for the most part unsuccessfully, used by the members of the populist movement when they endeavored to approach the peasants.

Y. M.I. Drei (standing second from the right), a member of the Narodnaya Volya. Condemned in 1883, he spent fifteen years of forced labor in the Kara gold mines before his final release in 1898.

eighteenth century, and later of gold), soldiers, administrators—and, of course, convicts and exiles. Many non-Russians, however, were attracted to St. Petersburg and Moscow, and certain ethnic groups sometimes became associated with particular trades or professions there—Tatars from Kazan, for instance, worked as janitors or rag-and-bone merchants, and there were mosques in both cities for these and other Muslims. Despite a notable lack of racial—as distinct from religious—prejudice, there also seems to have been little intermixture through marriage, except in some areas of early colonization (Finns and Great Russians, for example, as already mentioned) or unstabilized borderlands and sometimes, in a statistically insignificant way, at the top of the social scale—there were unions, for example, between Russian and Caucasian aristocratic families, as well as some mingling of Tatar and Russian blue blood, particularly after the fall of Kazan in the sixteenth century, when a number of the Golden Horde's nobles converted to Orthodoxy and became Russified, leaving only their names as witness to the partially Tatar origin of several of Russia's first families. (Otherwise, however, there is scarcely any literal substance to Napoleon's famous dictum that "if you scratch a Russian you will find a Tatar.")

Although they are not, strictly speaking, a separate race, special mention must be made of the Cossacks. They were a product of the vague nature of Russia's frontiers during the early days of her expansion toward the east and the south, when fluctuating fortunes of war with the Tatars created a no-man's-land in which adventurous spirits and fugitives could lead a free life, combining agriculture with border warfare. Many were runaway serfs from the central Russian areas or from the Polish-dominated southwest, but through intermarriage in the ethnically confused borderlands they developed into a fairly distinct type, though always remaining Russian or Ukrainian in language. By the very nature of their origins they were excellent fighters, but also rebellious ones, who could be fickle in their allegiance to one side or the other. In the final analysis, however, their Orthodoxy tended to make them loyal to Moscow, and they eventually lost their independence as a result. They played a vital part in the gradual extension of Russia's frontiers—it was a Cossack force, acting on its own initiative, which in the time of Ivan the Terrible broke residual Tatar resistance to the complete Russian conquest of Siberia. The best-known and largest Cossack settlements arose in the southern borderlands, along the lower reaches of the rivers Dnieper and Don—a location of considerable strategic advantage during the long-drawn-out triangular conflict between Poland, Muscovy and the Crimean Tatar vassals of Turkey. Until the later part of the seventeenth century the Ukrainian-speaking Cossacks on the Dnieper (called Zaporozhians, from the name of their headquarters "beyond the rapids") constituted a kind of independent republic which, although nominally under Polish suzerainty, effectively controlled the Ukraine for a while—only at this time did its people briefly enjoy something resembling national autonomy. During the eighteenth century both the Zaporozhians and the Don Cossacks were brought under firm Russian control, soon losing both their freedom and the rough democracy (under elected "atamans" or "hetmans") which went with it. Though the higher-ranking ones tended in the course of time to become assimilated into the Russian landowning officer class,

the Cossacks as a whole, in their prosperous villages on the Don and the Dnieper, remained a special community of yeoman farmers always ready to serve as cavalrymen in wartime. There were other Cossack settlements in the Caucasus on the rivers Kuban and Terek, and also in Siberia along the frontiers with China. In the later nineteenth and early twentieth centuries Cossack units were often used for the suppression of internal unrest, with the result that their earlier renown as dashing freebooters gave way to the unflattering image, in the public eye, of a brutal gendarmerie.

It remains to attempt a brief description of the state of Russian society as it had become by the middle of the last century—when some of the early photographs in this book were taken—and of the main developments in the ensuing period until the First World War. There were only four officially recognized classes (or "estates," as they were known): the gentry, the peasants, the clergy and the "townspeople." The last ill-defined category included artisans, merchants, cabdrivers and the like, and—as the towns grew in the latter half of the nineteenth century—it became, needless to say, the principal avenue of "upward mobility." Otherwise it was difficult to ascend the social scale, and there were also some specific prohibitions against transferring from one "estate" to another. Yet it is possible to exaggerate the rigidity of the system—"townspeople" were sometimes rewarded by ennoblement for services to the state, and by the end of the nineteenth century many peasants had joined the ranks of the "townspeople" as artisans, shopkeepers and factory workers—or factory owners. The distinguishing feature of the Russian system was not the existence of barriers between the classes, which were probably not much more impassable than elsewhere, but the fact that, for the historical reasons already noted, all were equally subordinate to the autocracy. It was only by virtue of service to the Czar that the gentry owned land and commanded the labor of the serfs who tilled it. It is true that Peter III, the ill-starred husband of Catherine the Great, in 1762 freed the gentry of the obligation to serve, but by this time it could make little difference: acceptance of autocratic rule had become ingrained, and though in many respects, as the mainstay of the civil administration and the army, the landed gentry in Russia seemed much the same as in the West, it had never aspired, as a class, to assert itself against the power of the sovereign. Court camarillas on occasion attempted to promote one candidate to the throne as against another—one unpopular czar, Paul I, was even assassinated—but members of the nobility never collectively challenged the autocracy as such, except in 1825, when a group of conspirators (the "Decembrists") made a confused attempt to upset the existing order in radical fashion. Their tragic rising was doomed to failure because it enjoyed neither the sympathy of the gentry as a whole, nor the effective support of the peasant soldiers vital to its success. Thereafter, individual noblemen who displayed reforming zeal in an undesirable direction were more than ever unceremoniously reminded of their basic lack of rights and, if sent to Siberia, would discover—as Dostoyevsky did—that their only remaining privilege was to be confined in better conditions than lower-class convicts. In terms of social and economic standing, members of the Russian gentry—as in other countries—differed very widely. In the higher range there were grand families, like the Sheremetevs, who owned palaces in St. Petersburg and vast country estates with thousands of "souls," as serfs were officially styled for fiscal purposes. On their estate near Moscow—and they were not alone in this—the Sheremetevs even maintained their own theaters, for which serfs were selected and trained as actors and singers. (A standard Russian word for "good-for-nothings" is *shantrapa,* derived from *chantera pas*—the comment uttered in the presence of a serf who failed his audition.) But Russian country gentlemen were much more typically impoverished, living in anything but luxury on run-down, often heavily mortgaged estates, and certainly in no position to provide for their own entertainment in such a lavish manner. As is clear enough from nineteenth-century literature, staving off taedium vitae was a major problem for landowners, sparsely dotted about as they were in a countryside notorious for its poor roads. Many, but not all, found distraction in some form of civil or military service which took them away from home at least in their more active years. But others retired early to what they may have hoped would be a life of contented sloth—which more commonly turned into one of frantic boredom. The Scottish traveler, Mackenzie Wallace, tells of a Russian country gentleman who *in extremis* used to have his servants waylay passersby on the nearest road and then forcibly subject them to his drunken company for several days before allowing them to proceed. Yet though there were enough Squire Westons among the Russian gentry to inspire such anecdotes, as well as the lampoons of satirists (themselves, mostly, of the gentry too), it must be said that this gentry also abundantly displayed the compensating virtues of a leisured class anywhere else. Apart from the fact that many of its members served their own country selflessly and with distinction, the world at large is likewise indebted to it for almost all of Russia's great writers and composers, and also for many of her scientists and scholars. Nor should it be forgotten that despite a general record of submission to the autocracy, the gentry produced numerous individual rebels—the army officers who staged the abortive insurrection mentioned above were landed aristocrats—and some outstanding apostles of political radicalism, among whom Bakunin and Kropotkin became internationally known and influential.

The mention of the word "serf" brings us to the social class which formed the broad base of the pyramid at whose apex stood the czar. Serfdom was not universal in the Russian empire. It scarcely existed in Siberia because by the time there was large-scale peasant settlement there it had been abolished. Neither was it an absolutely inescapable condition, since serfs could, and occasionally did, buy their freedom—or were sometimes manumitted. But it was the lot of the great majority on both private and state lands in the central Russian regions and most of the Ukraine. The peasants were not enserfed until the sixteenth century—before then they had been free to leave their masters every year, by tradition, on St. George's day in November. The introduction of serfdom meant that the peasants were bound to the land in the same way and for the same reasons as their masters were bound to the czar's service. During the eighteenth century, however, just as the privileges of the landowners were made absolute, so were the rights of their serfs whittled away until they became virtually slaves who could—and, notoriously, often were—bought and sold, even if it meant separating them from their families. Perhaps the very worst aspect of a serf's life was that—from the time of Peter the Great—he could be sent into the army for twenty-five years, for the young serfs of military age this was a

gruesome lottery, since a fixed quota had to be provided by every village, and the selection was often arbitrary, and could be vindictive. Of all the foreign words borrowed in Peter's time perhaps the most feared and hated was *rekrut.*

One of the crucial events in the nineteenth century was the emancipation of the serfs in 1861. It may well be that it was motivated mainly by economic and political self-interest—awareness of the inefficiency of serf labor and fear of increasing peasant turbulence if nothing was changed—but conscience also played its part: Russian literature is witness to the shame and embarrassment felt by some landowners at their almost unlimited powers over the peasants. If the gross abuse of these powers was the exception rather than the rule, so no doubt was the ideally patriarchal treatment of the peasants sometimes claimed in nostalgic retrospect—a sentimental memory occasionally shared even by ex-serfs, like the old family retainer in Chekhov's *Cherry Orchard* who believes the rot set in with "Freedom." In most cases, however, relations between masters and serfs were unhappy, morally and economically debilitating to both alike. After decades of inconclusive discussion about the need for emancipation Russia's defeat in the Crimean War finally made it inevitable. Yet the conservatives (many of them lesser landowners with few assets other than the serfs and their labor) were right to foresee that it would eventually lead to further radical changes of a more uncontrollable kind. While retaining its full powers, the autocracy was henceforth increasingly unable to prevent or inhibit the growth of autonomous social forces and found itself confronted by a dilemma resolved only by its own downfall in 1917. Its political decline was inevitable whether it acquiesced in or opposed the new trends. Like the hero of a well-known Russian ballad, the Czar would perish if he turned to the right at the crossroads—and also if he turned to the left. (The Czar who went furthest to the left, Alexander II—known as the "Liberator" because of his emancipation of the serfs—did literally perish at the hand of assassins, and the "reaction" of the two succeeding reigns must be seen in this light.) Attempts to achieve a constitutional compromise with irresistible forces of opposition in the early twentieth century only underlined the fact that Emancipation, by gradually blurring the lines of division in society through the creation of a relatively free market in labor, had unleashed new economic interests which could not easily be harnessed to the autocratic will in the name of expansion of national frontiers—a process which in any case had by now almost attained its natural limits. In other words, important elements in society for the first time began to assert themselves vis-à-vis the state, and thus implicitly to challenge the prevailing logic of Russian history, which had always previously seemed justifiable as the condition of sheer national survival, if in no other terms. It is true that the country had been no stranger to violent outbreaks of social unrest: there had been urban riots over economic grievances in the mid-seventeenth century, and savage mutinies on the turbulent outskirts of the empire, such as the Cossack Pugachev's rising in the reign of Catherine the Great. None of these, however, was directed against the autocracy as such—the aim of Pugachev's rebellion was actually to put himself, as the "legitimate" Czar, on the throne usurped by Catherine. The Decembrists of 1825 enjoyed no significant support from their own or any other class in society. Just as the beginnings of this basic change in the relations between Russian society and the state were precipitated by defeat in the Crimean War, so the first major political price for it was exacted about fifty years later by defeat in another war, this time with Japan, as the inevitable result of further reckless territorial expansion in the Far East. Widespread unrest and a naval mutiny in 1905 forced Nicholas II to grant a half-hearted Constitution and call an elective assembly, the Duma. This was an admirable body of its kind, representative, in its original form, of all social classes, and of the major national minorities, but it was bedeviled from the start by conflict with the autocracy as to the degree of its powers in legislation and over government.

Both before and after their emancipation the peasants, of course, constituted the overwhelming majority of the population, and once he left St. Petersburg the foreign traveler would rightly have felt that no country was more quintessentially rural. The poverty-stricken appearance of the countryside and the villages was often commented on by both foreign and Russian writers, and a common impression was that the peasants were sunk in squalor and ignorance. To many a passing visitor they seemed feckless, shifty, drunken and altogether besotted. In view of the extremely unfavorable climate—not to mention the effect of several centuries of serfdom—they could hardly have been expected to resemble the seemly and industrious cottagers of Western Europe (or at least of Western Europe's fond imagination!), but only a superficial observer would have failed to see that they were nevertheless the ultimate source—or at any rate the custodians—of many distinctive or original aspects of Russia's life and culture. This was acknowledged during the nineteenth century by educated, "Europeanized" Russians in a way that had no real parallel in the West. Their almost worshipful attitude to the peasantry may have been largely determined by the agonized sense of cultural isolation already mentioned—and it was liable to degenerate into mere silliness—but it was based on a recognition, moving even in its occasional excessiveness, of qualities that were justly felt to be possessed by no other people in quite the same degree. The testimony of Russian literature certainly suggests that the Russian peasants not only displayed the Christian virtues of charity, compassion and forbearance in unusual measure, but that they were also endowed with a natural sense of equality and justice (though not, alas, with the need to enforce it by law). This peasant egalitarianism may have been one of the few positive consequences of servitude, and it was embodied in a peculiar institution, the village commune (*mir*), which every few years redistributed among all peasant households the land available for their personal tillage, thus ensuring fair and equal treatment, and fostering a sense of co-ownership. The meetings of the *mir*, under an elected "elder," also instilled a feeling of collective responsibility for village affairs, and although it did not make for good farming, the existence of the commune encouraged a widespread belief in the later nineteenth century that there was a ready-made basis here for a form of popular socialism—at one time even Karl Marx was persuaded that Russia could thus achieve the millennium without going through a capitalist phase.

As can be seen from the many photographs of them, the peasants preserved in their very appearance a style that was unadulterated—at least until late in the nineteenth century—by European influences. They were invariably bearded (though they cut their hair in a rough

fashion) and wore homespun garments, of which the most characteristic was the red-dyed shirt or long smock. In winter they kept warm in sheepskin coats or kaftans of thick cloth. The women had colorful *sarafans* and on special occasions sometimes replaced their simple kerchiefs with a high embroidered headdress called a *kokoshnik*. Shoe leather was scarce and expensive, so footwear was generally plaited from strips of bark or other materials, including even horsehair, and boots were also rolled from felt. There was an ingenious self-sufficiency in everything—utensils and even plowshares were made of wood. Many everyday products of peasant skill demonstrated an affecting sense of beauty, or at least a need to relieve the drabness of life with color and decoration—as seen from astonishingly intricate fretwork carving on the outside of houses, embroidery, the painting of spoons and other wooden household objects. Among the many "cottage industries" in which whole villages sometimes specialized was icon-painting—that of Palekh being particularly remarkable. Russian folklore—fairy tales, songs and, in some areas, epic poems about a legendary pre-Muscovite past—was outstandingly rich and expressive, as one would expect from a people who had to while away long monotonous winter months in virtual idleness. The most impressive testimony to the collective genius of the peasantry is the Russian language itself. None other—not even the closely related Slav languages—can match it in its breathtaking resourcefulness. Its quality shows particularly in a wealth of pithy proverbs and sayings unrivaled anywhere else in Europe. As Turgenev said in a famous hymn of praise to it, "such a language can only have been given to a great people." The peasantry preserved it from the disastrous invasion by foreign words in the eighteenth century, and Russia's leading writers could count themselves fortunate in being able to draw on the bounties of unadulterated popular speech. The contribution of folk elements to the work of some nineteenth-century composers, such as Glinka, also testified to the debt which the national culture owed to the peasants.

As was, of course, foreseeable, Emancipation created as many problems as it solved if not more. The peasants were given the freedom that the majority had undoubtedly yearned for ever since it had been taken away in the sixteenth century. It was, however, a very conditional freedom. To an important extent the peasants were now their own masters as regards the disposal of their labor, but they still had to have the permission of the communes before leaving their native villages, and—the most grievous limitation—they were required to pay compensation to the gentry for the land they had always, as serfs, tilled on their own account. A peasant who went to work in the towns, as many now did, would still have to pay this through his commune, which, as before, had responsibility in such matters for all its members, even if they were absent. (When this huge peasant "debt" eventually got hopelessly in arrears it was simply canceled by government decree in the early twentieth century.) There were many new causes of antagonism—too numerous and complex to be detailed here—between the ex-serf and his former master, and Emancipation did anything but initiate an era of harmony in the countryside. One particularly sore point was that woodland on the estates was no longer so easily accessible to the peasants. The landowners, whose own economic decline continued apace, naturally wished to capitalize on this valuable asset, and the peasants were always trying to steal it from them—the need of the northern Russian peasant for wood to heat the large brick stove on which he and his family slept during the long cold winter was insatiable. (In the southern steppe regions, where there was little timber, dry dung—called *kizyak*—was commonly used as domestic fuel.) These difficulties were compounded during the second half of the nineteenth century by a rapid growth in the rural population and a consequent shortage of good land—which was not relieved by the extensive "opening up" of Siberia for peasant settlement until too late, alas, to help avert the social and political disasters to come. Agriculture stagnated, and in many northern and central regions there was visible impoverishment. As can be seen from some of the photographs, individual landowners and peasants tried to modernize and diversify farming on their land by introducing machinery, but a general shortage of capital for agricultural investment restricted the scope of such ventures. Only in the "black earth" south did more efficient large-scale farming produce a surplus of wheat for export, which accounted for much of the trade that passed through such flourishing Black Sea ports as Odessa and Novorossiisk. The poor, perennially underfertilized soil of the north, on the other hand, continued to yield little more than subsistence crops, such as the rye from which the peasant baked his staple black bread, oats for his horse, and the flax from which his clothes were made. It also supported the cultivation of such vitamin-providers as cucumber and cabbage, the pickling of which was essential to the maintenance of life during the winter—hence the great importance in the peasant economy of salt (which, like the other great sustainer, vodka, was a state monopoly). Side by side with agricultural decline in some areas went another inevitable consequence of Emancipation—economic differentiation among the peasants. In the same commune it was possible for a minority to grow richer by acquiring additional land, and by hiring the labor of their poorer fellow villagers. In theory this could and did, in individual cases, make for better agriculture, with the less efficient being overtaken by the more enterprising. But the moral loss to the peasantry as a whole soon became depressingly apparent—to judge in particular by the less flattering portrayal of peasants to be found in the literature of the later nineteenth and early twentieth centuries (in some stories and plays of Chekhov, for example). Even without this literary evidence, it could be assumed that, with expanding opportunities for individual advancement or self-enrichment—whether still on the land or through migration to the towns—the all too human qualities of rapacity, greed and envy were bound to make their inroads. The commune, once the locus of a peculiar kind of rural democracy, tended now to be restricted more to its function as a tax-collecting mechanism—the aspect that had always chiefly recommended it to the authorities.

Emancipation was followed shortly by other reforms which also contributed importantly to the "modernization" of Russian society. The first of these was a new legal system. Justice had always been administered in rough-and-ready fashion by landowners or officials, and the dominant factors which in Russian history had militated against any effective challenge to the autocratic power had also been highly unpropitious not only to the emergence of proper legal institutions, but also to the cultivation of a sense of law. When, on a visit to the Inns of Court in London, Peter the Great was informed that the bewigged gentlemen who met his astonished gaze were lawyers, he is supposed to have said, "I have only one such scoundrel in the whole of my empire—and him I mean to hang when I return!" (He was better pleased by Woolwich Arsenal, where, in the words of a contemporary English account, "he did himself in the throwing of bombs assay.") Whether true or false, this story well illustrates the kind of tradition that has led students of Russia to doubt that a rule of law could ever take root there. But the new legal institutions introduced in the 1860's functioned well enough, by all accounts. They were a workable compromise between the French and the English systems, and provided for trial by jury. It is true that the independence of the Russian judiciary could be overriden in political cases—and serious interference began nearly fifteen years after the reform, though not without severe provocation, when a would-be terrorist assassin, whose guilt was beyond doubt, was acquitted by a jury. The main criticism of the post-Reform legal system was, in fact, that the juries tended to be far too lenient, and that it was therefore difficult to obtain convictions in criminal cases, whether or not they had a political aspect. This was probably indicative as much of traditional Russian sympathy for the unfortunate as of automatic opposition to the authorities, or of indifference to law as such. Even so, service on juries undoubtedly gave many Russians of all classes (including peasants) a taste for "due process" which in time was bound to lead to a more widespread understanding that legal formality is not incompatible with justice and mercy. By the twentieth century it was possible to obtain an excellent legal training at Russian universities, and the bar was a respected calling which attracted people of outstanding ability (Alexander Kerensky, who became head of the Provisional Government in July 1917 after the fall of the monarchy in February of that year, began his career as a defense lawyer, sometimes handling the cases of members of the party which later, in October 1917, ousted him from power—and then proceeded to demolish the fragile foundation of both law and democracy in Russia.)

The creation of a new legal system only underlined the fact that Russia was still basically—though henceforth much less arbitrarily—ruled by an officialdom almost entirely drawn, except at its lower levels, from the gentry. While England was moved to reform her civil service after the Crimean War, no such thing happened in Russia, where an elaborate hierarchy of fourteen grades, with exact equivalencies between civil and military ranks, retained overriding powers as the instrument of the czar's will. Like so much else in post-Muscovite Russia, it had been established by Peter the Great, and was decked out with grandiloquent titles and imposing uniforms, both largely inspired by German models. With their reputation for venality, particularly in the provinces, Russian officials were not well loved, and were the favorite butt of satirists, yet some were cultivated and humane, and they perhaps hardly deserved to be reduced to the lowest common denominator of the bribe-takers and martinets in their midst. ("There's only one decent man," remarks a character of Gogol, "in this town—the public prosecutor—and he's a swine!") However, even if they had all been paragons of virtue, the trouble was that they were neither numerous nor competent enough to manage the affairs of such a vast territory, and after Emancipation the practical need for ways of improving the administration became glaringly obvious. It was met to some extent by shifting a good deal of responsibility for local affairs in the countryside—road and bridge building, health, schools, etc.—to newly created elective assemblies called *zemstvos* (similar bodies—in effect, municipal councils—were set up in the towns a little later). Despite their admitted limitations and chronic lack of funds, these not only made tangible improvements in rural life, but also gave invaluable lessons in the theory and practice of self-government— little wonder that in the upheaval of 1905 they emerged as a considerable force on the side of parliamentarism. The franchise for *zemstvo* elections was weighted in favor of the gentry, but there were also peasant members—which meant that, for the first time in Russian history, there was a forum for open debate on matters of common concern between representatives of the two classes always socially most divided from each other.

The last but not least important—and perhaps most overdue—of the reforms was that of the army, which was introduced eighteen years after the end of the Crimean War. The cruel selective levy of peasant youths was abolished and replaced by universal conscription. The term of service was reduced from twenty-five years to six at the most. It was altogether more equitable and just, providing for exemptions on an eminently rational basis: university students were not called up—though they could volunteer as privates—nor were the only sons of peasants.

Thanks to the spontaneous and eventually fateful movements it set in train, the most significant development in the post-Emancipation era was the rapid expansion of industry—henceforth nourished by an inflow of "free" labor from the villages. The overall direction of economic policy remained in the hands of the state, but even though its interests often coincided with those of the private entrepreneurs (increased production of textiles and steel, for instance, was obviously of mutual benefit), the government became increasingly concerned by the difficulty of controlling or regulating the thrusting new energies released by this inevitable and essential process. The dilemma was reflected in a conflict during the later nineteenth century between the czar's Ministry of Finance, which put the emphasis on encouragement for industrialization, and his Ministry of the Interior, which was justifiably alarmed at the social consequences. Ironically, the emancipated peasantry not only supplied the labor force required by industrial growth, but also made a significant contribution to the entrepreneurial drive behind it. In itself this was not something entirely new. It had always been possible for a small trickle of peasants to "better" themselves by becoming artisans or merchants: long before Emancipation some managed to buy or were granted their freedom, and went off to seek their fortune in the towns, or else stayed at home to engage in a lucrative trade or craft; others, while remaining serfs, could work as artisans on condition that they paid a regular "quit-fee" to their masters—a welcome source of cash for those whose land was unproductive. Since this often occurred in central and northern areas, Moscow and St. Petersburg always had a ready source of manpower for their incipient industries in the early nineteenth century. Serf labor could also simply be switched from agriculture to industry: as already noted, the first Russian ordnance factories under Peter the Great were manned by serfs, and later on it was not unknown for private owners of factories or mines to *buy* the serfs needed to operate them. After Emancipation the trickle of peasant

recruitment to industry developed, if not into a flood, at least into a steadily broadening stream, and with the beginnings of investment banking—and also thanks to an influx of foreign capital and managerial skill—rapid growth was guaranteed. For French, British, Belgian, Swedish and other investors, Russia was an attractive proposition. Apart from relatively cheap (if not always very experienced) labor, there were infinite natural resources to be exploited: ubiquitous timber, oil in Baku (from which Alfred Nobel made part of his fortune), gold and other minerals in Siberia, coal and iron in the Donets basin—here the main town was founded in 1870 by a Welshman, John Hughes, and named Yuzovka in his honor. By the end of the century a previous heavy dependence on river transport, with its seasonal stoppages, had been much reduced by a boom in railroad construction. All this enhanced the country's potential for economic "take-off." Despite such limitations as the continuing primacy of the autocracy's strategic and political considerations over mere commercial ones, and the relative timidity of native capital, Russia could anticipate giant industrial expansion. Indeed, in the twentieth century, before the First World War, she compared favorably with the advanced Western countries in her rate of economic growth (though not of course in actual volume of output). It is possible, judging by her advance toward truly constitutional government in the aftermath of the war with Japan, that she would also have found an appropriate means of mitigating the social cost of this progress in much the same way as Western industrial nations did. But with the further disastrous war which began in 1914, time suddenly ran out, and the blandishments of revolution understandably proved seductive to an army consisting largely of peasants whose loyalty and age-old capacity to endure had been strained beyond any reasonable measure.

It was at first sight a peculiar feature of the Russian "road to capitalism" that not only the new working class but also many of the entrepreneurs (themselves, as already mentioned, often of serf origin) should have been a source of disaffection in the last decades of imperial rule. Despite a certain amount of protective factory legislation, the uprooted peasants living in squalid, overcrowded slums or bleak industrial barracks on the outskirts of St. Petersburg, Moscow and other cities had obvious reasons for discontent, having lost even the rudimentary social security offered by the commune or extended family in the villages. Although by the turn of the century they were still a small proportion—under three million—of the total population, their concentrated proximity to the seats of power justified the Marxist view of them as the social force with the highest revolutionary potential; and working-class unrest in the two capitals indubitably played a part, even if not a crucial one, in bringing down the monarchy. For their part, the emergent Russian capitalists—who were particularly active in the old, established textile industry and in the manufacture of sugar from beet—showed growing impatience with a bureaucratic, *dirigiste* regime which inhibited the full application of their bursting energies. It was natural that many of them should have hankered after a political remedy, and in the elections to the Duma after the Constitution of 1905 they mostly supported the liberal "Cadet" (Constitutional Democrat) party, whose eventual contribution to ending the autocratic rule was certainly more decisive than that of either of the two rival revolutionary movements (the Social Democrats, split after

1903 into Mensheviks and Bolsheviks, who put their faith in the proletariat, and the Social Revolutionaries, who looked rather to the peasantry). Some leading Russian industrialists expressed their discontent or relieved their consciences in other ways: the textile magnate Savva Morozov, for instance, gave handsome subsidies to the Bolsheviks, and there are well-vouched-for stories of Russian capitalists fomenting strikes in their own factories (a good portrait of a "progressive" Russian tycoon is that of Kologrivov in Boris Pasternak's *Doctor Zhivago*). Yet others distinguished themselves by enlightened welfare policies in the treatment of their workers. There were no doubt many more who were mean, narrow-minded and grasping in the tradition of the ingrown merchant world from which part of the new capitalist class derived, but on the whole the nouveaux riches of St. Petersburg and Moscow enjoyed a reputation for generosity, and also for exhibiting the kind of wild impulsiveness, flamboyance and spontaneity which, Russians had good reason to feel, distinguished them from the straitlaced Western European "bourgeois." Illustrative anecdotes abound: one memoirist, for example, relates how a certain Moscow tycoon issued a standing invitation to all his friends and associates to join him every morning for "elevenses"—at which the champagne ceased to be served only when his top hat, placed upside down on a table, could hold no more corks from the bottles emptied in rapid succession. At a more exalted level, such openhandedness was beginning to manifest itself by the end of the nineteenth century in patronage and art collecting on a scale and in a manner which compared favorably with those of any Western country. Most notable perhaps was Sergei Shchukin, who in the early twentieth century attended the *salons* in Paris where he personally selected and bought many paintings by Picasso and Matisse (all now in a Moscow art gallery).

Finally, a little must be said about two other groups in Russian society: the clergy and the intelligentsia (the latter was not officially recognized as a separate class). It may seem incongruous to bracket these together—though not, perhaps, if one considers that both, in their different ways, contended for the soul of the nation, and that some outstanding members of the intelligentsia were actually sons of priests. The Russian Church has often been criticized for its submissiveness to secular authority; it should be remembered, however, that of all the social groups or institutions which at one time or another might have withstood the overriding claims of the autocracy, the Church was the least well placed to do so—partly, indeed, because of the very nature of its teaching (with a particular emphasis in Orthodoxy, furthermore, on the supreme importance of meekness and humility). Even so, its total subordination to the temporal power came comparatively late: only in the eighteenth century, when Peter the Great—not for nothing widely regarded as Anti-Christ in person—abolished the Patriarchate, and put the Church under the control of a body called the Holy Synod, which, though composed of clergy, was always in effect controlled by a lay official. Catherine the Great completed its humiliation by confiscating the extensive land holdings of the monasteries—which had supported the Church as a whole—and virtually making the priests into salaried servants of the state. But despite this double blow, the Church continued to exercise its ministry as an inseparable part of the daily life of the great majority of the population. It may be that the learning of the average village priest scarcely extended

beyond mere literacy and that the deeper spiritual needs of many simple souls were more readily satisfied by the sects that arose out of the Schism (and later by some protestant movements of foreign inspiration); the Church nonetheless remained the chief visible repository and guardian of the country's millennial traditions, and, for most people, was of course the only source of mystery and ritual in an existence which would otherwise have been intolerably cheerless. The very beauty of the Russian churches (with their gilded or brightly painted cupolas and whitewashed walls they were generally the only brick or stone buildings, and often stood where possible on higher ground overlooking the gray, straggling wooden villages), the magnificence of the choral singing, the rich vestments of the priests, the solemn processions with banners on the many feast days, the icons, lamps and lighted candles—all this could scarcely fail to inspire awe, if not piety. As in the Greek Church, priests were allowed to marry—which meant that the clergy was largely a self-perpetuating hereditary calling—and, in general, led a life similar to that of their parishioners, even working on the land allotted to them. The Church hierarchy, on the other hand, was celibate and drawn from among the so-called black clergy, that is, the monks. By comparison with Western churches, the Russian one was not very active in proselytization or education. There were some missions to pagan tribes in Siberia and Alaska, and attempts were made to counter Catholic and Protestant influence in the western areas where it was particularly strong—some Latvian and Estonian peasants, for example, were converted to Orthodoxy, and Ukrainian Uniates reconverted to it. Otherwise the Russian Church was fairly tolerant of other denominations, and there was at least one case of it allowing non-Orthodox missionary work among Muslims in the empire—by Scottish Presbyterians in the Caucasus. The Church attended to its own education more than is sometimes appreciated—there were four major "Spiritual Academies" which carried on theological studies at a higher level, and some youths were trained for the priesthood at seminaries—particularly in the southwest, where, owing to the long Polish domination, a somewhat incongruous emphasis was put on the study of Latin. Although it arose in part outside the Church, an impressive corpus of speculative religious thought in the works of some writers (including Dostoyevsky) in the later nineteenth and early twentieth centuries demonstrated that Russian Orthodoxy was capable of an intellectual vigor certainly no less than that of the secular systems of belief which competed with it. An important aspect of Russian religious life was the virtually professional pilgrims referred to as "wanderers" who roamed the country in large numbers, supporting themselves by the alms always forthcoming among an exceptionally charitable population. These were a good embodiment of perhaps one of the most outstanding features of the Russian spirit—a restlessness which often drove people of all social classes to set off in search of the ever-elusive combination of truth and justice summed up in the untranslatable word *pravda* (and now, alas, appropriated as its title by the world's most mendacious newspaper).

This spiritual restlessness was also well exemplified by the intelligentsia. It is, of course, significant that the term itself has been borrowed from Russian into English, being rightly felt to have a peculiar sense not easily conveyed by any approximate Western equivalent. Needless to say, until Emancipation higher education at the eighteenth-century University of Moscow and later at others (such as those of St. Petersburg, Kazan and Kiev), founded in the nineteenth century, was largely, but not exclusively, restricted to members of the gentry class, and it was certainly only they who had the means and the leisure to devote themselves to cultural pursuits—though often concurrently with some form of civil or military service. Not surprisingly, too, the first expressions of intellectual discontent with the status quo arose in the same milieu. But in a country where only the limitless expanse of its territory could match the enormity of the social problems bequeathed by its history, it was understandable that the contemplation of them by a small educated elite, culturally isolated from the great mass of the nation and deprived of any say in its government, should frequently have induced anguish, or even despair. Hard put to it to conceive of a way out for which they might personally work with any expectation of success, many felt both guiltily frustrated and hopelessly out of place. The figure of the so-called superfluous man, followed after Emancipation by that of the "penitent nobleman," occupied a central place in nineteenth-century literature. With the ruthless candor typical of it, this literature also shows how easily undirected concern for the fate of Russia—and then, since there was nothing to be done about this, for the whole of mankind—could spend itself in fatuous talk, heroic posturing or sheer humbug. An inevitable result of this feeling of being in limbo was that the intelligentsia engaged in a constant search for all-embracing formulas or systems of ideas which might seem to provide not only a complete view of the world, but also a total solution to all its problems. This is the reason for the almost incredible ferment produced in Russia by German philosophy. The excogitations of Schelling, Hegel, Fichte (and later Marx) were received as intoxicating revelations and stirred debate of a passion which might well have startled their authors. (Eager translations of such writings also had a disastrous effect on the style of Russian abstract prose.) The idea of trial and error, of piecemeal progress, had little appeal. Alexander Herzen, one of the most judicious nineteenth-century Russian thinkers, poked kindly fun at the intelligentsia's hunger for maximalist panaceas in a novel with the symptomatic title *Who Is to Blame?* His hero, a young nobleman who goes to study medicine in Germany, dazzles everyone with his brilliance and wit, but when it comes to the humdrum business of anatomy classes, he lets it be known that he is not interested in finding a cure for the common cold—only in discovering a way of making men immortal. But this undeniably quixotic streak in the Russian intelligentsia was, on the whole, a function of an altruistic devotion to ideas and to visions of social betterment scarcely equaled in intensity anywhere in Western Europe, and frequently accompanied, moreover, by a disarming capacity for merciless self-examination. In the few years before Emancipation, and particularly afterwards, with the gradual broadening of educational opportunities to include greater numbers of commoners, a tougher, more assertive generation came to put its imprint on the intelligentsia. As we see from Turgenev's novel *Fathers and Sons* the cultivated, well-bred scions of landowning families found themselves challenged by the sons of clerks, minor officials, priests, country doctors (still a very lowly calling) and others whose only social advantage over the peasantry was an ability to read and write. These newcomers put their faith in the natural sciences

and in the promise of a quick salvation held out by the positivist view of life which seemed to flow from them. Having no time for art, poetry or the amenities of life, they were proud to be called "nihilists" by their critics, and they joined the intelligentsia in sufficient numbers to bring about a distinct coarsening of its grain in the sixties and seventies, a period which also saw the beginnings of a revolutionary terrorism destined to become endemic. At their worst, individual members of the intelligentsia could certainly be as boorish and nasty as those portrayed in Dostoyevsky's *The Possessed*, but they were hardly representative of the majority. At the beginning of the twentieth century a significant group of intellectuals (among them Nicholas Berdyaev) revolted against the philosophical utilitarianism of the previous generation, and severely criticized the intelligentsia as a whole for its immoderacy and self-willed isolation from society at large.

The attention attracted by the intelligentsia in its specific sense of a caste or corporation alienated from, yet bent on changing, society should not obscure the fact that by the beginning of this century the greatly expanded educational system was turning out a good number of doctors, engineers, lawyers, schoolteachers and other professional people. These, while they might individually, if only by virtue of radical inclinations, have felt to belong to the intelligentsia, were nonetheless mainly concerned with getting on with their jobs, and in the course of busy careers could easily drift away from it. Members of the gentry impoverished by Emancipation and forced to sell their land were an important source of recruits to the new professional class. (Educated persons or intellectuals of "reactionary" or even simply moderate or neutral political views scarcely qualified as members of the intelligentsia in its proper sense.) Not everybody had the time or stamina to sit up half the night in earnest debate to the accompaniment of endless cigarettes and glasses of tea—not to mention that at certain periods, particularly after the assassination of Alexander II, any resulting activities could bring trouble with the police, or arrest and exile to Siberia. It seems likely that in the course of time the intelligentsia in the special sense of the word would eventually have dwindled proportionally to form, as in the West, a relatively small minority of the educated or professional community as a whole. In the end, however, it was destroyed by the revolution it had so ardently desired and worked for—but which turned out, tragically, to be of stuff very different from that of the intelligentsia's generous dreams.

By the end of the nineteenth century academic standards at the universities in Russia were probably as high as anywhere in Europe, and Russians had already made fundamental contributions to science and learning (Lobachevsky in mathematics, for example, and Mendeleyev in chemistry, to name only two), but schooling was still woefully inadequate. Census figures showed that at the turn of the century less than a quarter of the population was able to read—though this figure disguised enormous regional variations, ranging from almost universal literacy in the Baltic States to an almost equally total absence of it in Central Asia. Ever since Peter the Great had founded institutions of higher learning without bothering to create at the same time elementary and secondary schools, Russian education had been notably top-heavy. It was only after Emancipation that obsessive official fears of the consequences of educating the peasantry were to some extent abated, with the result that the number of schools in the villages began to increase rapidly. This process was aided by the newly created local government bodies *(zemstvos)* and by the Church, which was encouraged to open more parish schools in the hope that the harmful proclivities thought inseparable from book learning might thus be held in check. However, even if a peasant now had a better chance of learning the three R's, it was still very hard for him—partly for understandable economic reasons, and partly owing to less excusable official policy—to climb the educational ladder any higher. He would be lucky to get into a trade school and thence graduate more smoothly into the rising urban class of artisans and skilled workers. By and large, access to secondary education—including some excellent private schools—continued to be weighted in favor of the gentry; however, persons of humbler origin, particularly in the towns, were not ipso facto excluded, and in view of the uncommon talents or persistence needed to cross the hurdles other than by luck, there tended to be a natural self-selection of persons of exceptional quality from the lower classes, and by the twentieth century it was not unknown for university professors to be of peasant stock. (Secondary schools were modeled on German lines, with an emphasis on Greek and Latin which, as elsewhere, was as stultifying to some as it was enriching to others, but in the second half of the nineteenth century it became increasingly easier to opt for modern languages and science in nonclassical and commercial schools.) Education for women was at first slow in developing at any level, but here, too, in the later nineteenth century, there was surprisingly rapid progress, particularly after the establishment in the 1870's of "Higher Courses for Women" at Moscow and St. Petersburg universities. In this way—and also through study abroad—a growing number of Russian women were able to qualify for the medical, legal and teaching professions. There were no specific restrictions on the entry of non-Russians into secondary schools and universities, except in the case of Jews—but even this was far from being a total ban; though they were officially limited to a very small percentage of the student body by the so-called *numerus clausus*, a significant number nevertheless received higher education during the latter half of the nineteenth century, and some went on to occupy high academic posts—as, for instance, the father of Boris Pasternak. (Official discrimination against Jews was, incidentally, on religious, not racial, grounds, and a Jew could escape his legal disabilities by converting to Russian Orthodoxy.)

A good reason for dwelling on education at the end of this outline of prerevolutionary Russian history and society is that the old regime is often judged to have been particularly negligent in its provision of opportunities in this area, and hence to have been doomed to stagnation, or at least to have been incapable of social progress as understood in the West. A backward glance at mid-Victorian England might, however, suffice to suggest that, at least in the light of such a comparison, the Russia of the czars was not as hopelessly benighted or resistant to change as is often thought. The photographs that follow make it clear that the same held true of other fields—and by vividly conjuring up in immediate images before our eyes a vanished era in Russian life, perhaps they may also help guard against the "cranberries" to which we foreigners are always so liable whenever we rely on mere words.

The following books, all of which were extremely helpful in the writing of the above introductory essay, may be recommended for further background reading:

Robert Auty and Dimitri Obolensky (eds.), *Companion to Russian Studies: An Introduction to Russian History* (Cambridge, 1976). Concise and reliable essays by various hands on all the main periods.

Karl Baedecker, *Russia: A Handbook for Travellers* (London and New York, 1914; reissued by the original London publishers in 1971). This famous guidebook can still be browsed in with profit for useful tidbits of information; invaluable plans and descriptions of towns, particularly of Moscow, make it possible to trace important buildings or whole areas later demolished.

Edward Crankshaw, *The Shadow of the Winter Palace: The Drift to Revolution, 1905–1917* (London, 1976). A superbly written narrative, full of insight into the personalities of the last four czars, and on the historical factory which led to "the suicide of the monarchy."

Richard Pipes, *Russia under the Old Regime* (New York, 1974). An erudite study of the mainsprings of Russian history with particularly stimulating chapters on the various social classes. There are some striking photographs, as well as reproductions of old prints and engravings which give a good idea of the country in the pre-photographic era.

Nicholas V. Riasanovsky, *A History of Russia*, 3rd ed. (London and New York, 1963). An excellent general survey from Kievan times to the present day.

Hugh Seton-Watson, *The Russian Empire, 1801–1917* (London and New York, 1967). A judicious and highly readable account based on a thorough study of primary sources; sympathetic in the best sense both to the Russians and to the peoples they ruled over.

Andrey Sinyavsky (Abram Tertz), *A Voice from the Chorus* (London and New York, 1976). Apart from the passage quoted in the introductory essay, these notes written during the author's imprisonment contain other profound reflections on the spirit of Russian history and culture.

Sir Donald Mackenzie Wallace: *Russia on the Eve of War and Revolution* (New York, 1961). A classic account of the state of Russia in the later nineteenth and early twentieth centuries by a correspondent of the London *Times* who lived and traveled widely in the country during the reigns of the last three czars. Probably no Westerner in modern times came to know Russia so intimately, and certainly none has ever written on the subject with such grace, lucidity and common sense. The first edition appeared in 1877, and updated ones in 1905 and 1912. It is now most easily available in a paperback (Vintage) edition.

In addition to the above, mention should be made of two recently published photographic surveys:

Kyril FitzLyon and Tatiana Browning, *Before the Revolution* (London, 1977). Covers the reign of Nicholas II and includes a valuable introduction.

Marvin Lyons, *Nicholas II, the Last Tsar* (New York, 1975). A collection of nineteenth- and early-twentieth-century photographs.

1.

ST. PETERSBURG

ST. PETERSBURG

$\mathcal{S}$ T. PETERSBURG, THE NEW CAPITAL, was founded at the beginning of the eighteenth century by Peter the Great. More than forty thousand men toiled at the construction of the new city, "the window onto Europe," built on the Finnish marshlands of the Ladoga region, at the mouth of the Neva. The magnificence of the architecture and the spectral beauty of its rivers, quaysides and canals contributed to the ambiguous image of the city, at once stately and ghostly, "the brother of water and sky," in the words of the poet Mandelstam.

It was to become the greatest and most conspicuous outward token of the new Europeanized Russia. The official residence of the Emperor, the seat of the court and the administrative center of the empire, St. Petersburg was by the turn of the century a city of modern West European appearance with a population of some two million, one of the country's leading manufacturing towns and the most important commercial port on the Baltic Sea.

Preceding spread, 1. An early view of St. Petersburg, showing the Neva and the Fortress and Cathedral of St. Peter and St. Paul. Built by Trezzini in the first quarter of the eighteenth century, the cathedral was used as a burial place for Russian emperors since Peter the Great. The fortress, built as Peter's bastion against the Swedes, was later used as a prison.

2. Statue of Nicholas I by Baron P. K. Klodt.

Overleaf, 3. The Cathedral of the Smolny Convent, built in the mid-eighteenth century by Bartolomeo Rastrelli. The photograph was taken by Roger Fenton on his first trip to Russia in 1852.

4. The Winter Palace, the official residence of the Emperor, seen from the Neva. Begun in 1754, it is one of the finest examples of Bartolomeo Rastrelli's Baroque style. During the last reign it was used almost exclusively for state and social occasions; both the Emperor and the Empress preferred to live in the more informal atmosphere of the Alexander Palace at Tsarskoye Selo, some fifteen miles away from the capital.

5. The arch of the General Staff building, designed and built between 1819 and 1829 by Carlo Rossi. The arch, opening onto the Winter Palace Square, faces the Alexander Column, which was commissioned by Nicholas I in 1834 to commemorate Alexander I's victory over Napoleon. Hewn out of a single block of red granite, the column is 98 feet high and 13 feet in diameter. The total height of the monument is 153 feet.

6. Hay stacked on the Neva, with a factory in the background. *Fenton, 1852.*

7. Kazan Cathedral. Commissioned by the Emperor Paul, it was built in the reign of his successor, Alexander I, by A. Voronikhin and was modeled on St. Peter's and the Pantheon in Rome. At present it houses the Museum of the History of Religion and Atheism.

8. Construction work on the left bank of the Neva, c. 1870. To the right stand the Winter Palace and the Admiralty. The latter, founded by Peter the Great and remodeled by A. Zakharov between 1806 and 1823, was famed for the gilded spire which surmounted its 230-foot-high tower.

9. The Empress Maria Feodorovna with the future Emperor Nicholas II, c. 1873.

10. Maria Feodorovna with her two daughters, Xenia and Olga, on a formal occasion, probably on board the imperial yacht, c. 1892.

11. The Emperor Alexander III, the Empress Maria Feodorovna and her sister, Queen Alexandra of England, on a family visit to the King and Queen of Denmark, c. 1880.

12. The Emperor and the Empress surrounded by officers of the Regiment of Cavalier Guards, c. 1904.

13. Emperor Franz Joseph of Austria on a state visit to St. Petersburg in May 1897, with Nicholas II at his side.

14. Maneuvers and military review at the Guards' summer camp at Krasnoye Selo, c. 1908.

Following the Revolution of 1905, the Duma, or legislative chamber, was instituted by the imperial manifesto of October 17 through the efforts of S. Yu. Witte, then president of the Council of Ministers. It was intended by the liberal elements in the country to become the organ of constitutional government. Its powers, however, were restricted from the start by the fact that the ministers, appointed by the Emperor, were directly responsible to him and not to the Duma. Increasingly sharp conflicts with the government led to its early dissolution by the Emperor in July 1906—an experience which was to be repeated several times before its final disappearance in 1917. This experiment in constitutional government was, in the words of a modern historian, "too much and too late."

The largest party in the first Duma were the Kadets (Constitutional Democrats), drawn in the main from the educated classes, followed by the Labor Group (Trudoviki), which included peasants, industrial workers, minor officials and schoolteachers.

15. Preparing the elections in the St. Petersburg City Hall.

16. Voting for candidates.

17. The ethnic composition of the imperial Duma reflected the variety of populations within the empire. Alongside the Great Russians, who formed the majority, were Ukrainians, White Russians, Poles, Lithuanians, Letts, Estonians, Germans, Jews, Tatars and Bashkirs. There were also deputies from the Mordva, the Votyaks, the Chuvash, the Circassians and the Kalmyks. Muslim members numbered thirty.

18. A group of delegates representing various professions.

Overleaf, 19. The Emperor Nicholas II delivering his "speech from the throne" on May 10, 1906, in St. George's Hall in the Winter Palace. Placed near him are the imperial insignia, the crown, the mantle, the scepter and the staff, brought to St. Petersburg from Moscow. Two high court officials hold the imperial standard and the sword. In the left-hand corner stand the two empresses surrounded by their ladies-in-waiting. In the foreground (on the right facing the throne) are the delegates to the Duma and (on the left) members of the State Council.

15. 16. 17. 18.

20. The troubled year of 1905 left an aftermath of unrest. A street scene in St. Petersburg in 1906.

20.

MOSCOW

MOSCOW

OSCOW, THE "ANCIENT CAPITAL" popularly known as the "white stone city," retained after the founding of St. Petersburg its status for ceremonial occasions. It is here that the czars were crowned, and it was in the little chapel of the Iberian Virgin at the Voskresenskaya Gate (which led into the Red Square) that the Emperor, when he visited Moscow, would pray before entering the Kremlin.

Built on seven hills rising gently from the banks of the Moskva, the city did not become the actual center of the newly united Russian state until the fifteenth century, under Ivan III, a position it held until the early eighteenth century. Although much of it was destroyed by fire in 1812 during the war with Napoleon, it was rapidly rebuilt and, unlike the new capital on the Neva, kept, at least in the eyes of its inhabitants, some of the hallowed traditions of Russia's past. Always closer to the life of the countryside, Moscow remained a home of the landed gentry, whose patriarchal traditions and more easygoing customs contrasted with the more bureaucratic, court-centered and cosmopolitan outlook of much of the St. Petersburg aristocracy.

By the turn of the century, Moscow, the center of a major railway network, with a population of about one and a half million, had become the industrial and commercial capital of the empire.

Preceding spread, 21. The Cathedral of St. Basil the Blessed in the Red Square. Built between 1554 and 1560 in the reign of Ivan IV to commemorate the recent capture of Kazan, it embodies in stone the main features of the wooden churches of northern Russia. Tradition has it that when the building was completed the Czar had the architects blinded to ensure that they produced no work of comparable beauty elsewhere. Its exuberant forms and brilliant coloring have often and wrongly been taken to illustrate the alleged "Oriental" element in early Russian architecture. *Fenton, 1852.*

22. The Czar Bell, measuring 26 feet in height and weighing 200 tons, is the world's largest bell. Its life was checkered and inglorious. Cast in 1735 at the behest of the Empress Anne, it was abandoned at birth in the foundry. Damaged by fire, it lay in the ground for a century, until the architect A. Monferrand managed to raise and transport it to its present site in 1836.

23. 24.   25.

23–25. Three photographs by Fenton, taken in the autumn of 1852, showing the Kremlin as seen from the Moskva, the gilded cupolas of the Kremlin cathedrals and a row of houses facing the monastery of the Savior. The wooden house in the left foreground is a *traktir*, or inn. These establishments were of various kinds, the grander serving caviar, sturgeon and other delicacies, while the more humble provided vast quantities of weak tea, black bread and salted cucumber.

Unpaved streets, like the one shown here, were still to be encountered at the beginning of this century.

26. The Lubyanskaya Square in the early 1880's. The archway is the Northern, or Vladimir, Gate of the Kitai-Gorod, which was adjacent to the Kremlin and comprised the Red Square. As early as the sixteenth century, the Kitai-Gorod was the main commercial center of Moscow.

26.

27. The interior of the Cathedral of the Dormition (Uspensky), rebuilt between 1475 and 1479 by the Italian architect Fioravanti and largely modeled on the twelfth-century cathedral of the same name in Vladimir. The name and form of this building illustrate the conscious effort of the Grand Princes of Moscow to assume the political and cultural heritage of Kievan Russia, and its Italian architects were hence obliged to conform to Byzantine principles of design. This five-domed cathedral became the coronation church of the rulers of Muscovy, a role it continued to play in the nineteenth century.

28. The cathedrals of the Archangel Michael and of the Annunciation. The former was designed by the Italian A. Novi in the early sixteenth century and served as the burial place for members of the Muscovite ruling family. The latter (late fifteenth century), reconstructed by Russian architects from Pskov, served as a royal chapel, where members of the Czar's family were baptized and married.

29. The iconostasis of the Church of the Savior, c. 1692.

30. Nicholas II leaving the Cathedral of the Dormition after his coronation on May 14, 1896.

Overleaf, *31.* The Grand Duchess Alexandra Iosifovna (seated) with members of the imperial family and attended by pages of the Corps des Pages, during the coronation ceremonies of 1896.

27. 28. 29. 30.

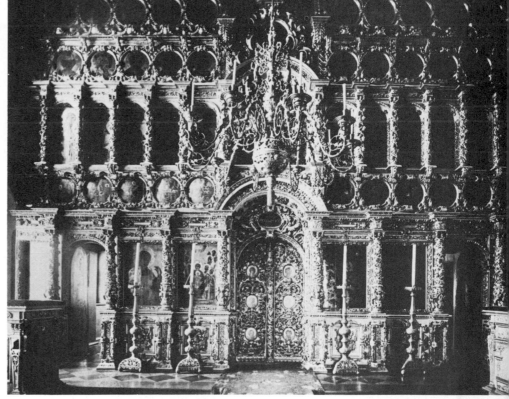

31.

32. Food and drink offered during the coronation festivities.

33, 34. The coronation procession of Nicholas II as it moved through the Kremlin and passed by the Faceted Palace (Granovitaya Palata), the former audience hall of the czars built in the late fifteenth century by Mario Ruffo and Pietro Antonio. During the nineteenth century it was used as a banquet hall, where the Czar, after the coronation, dined in state.

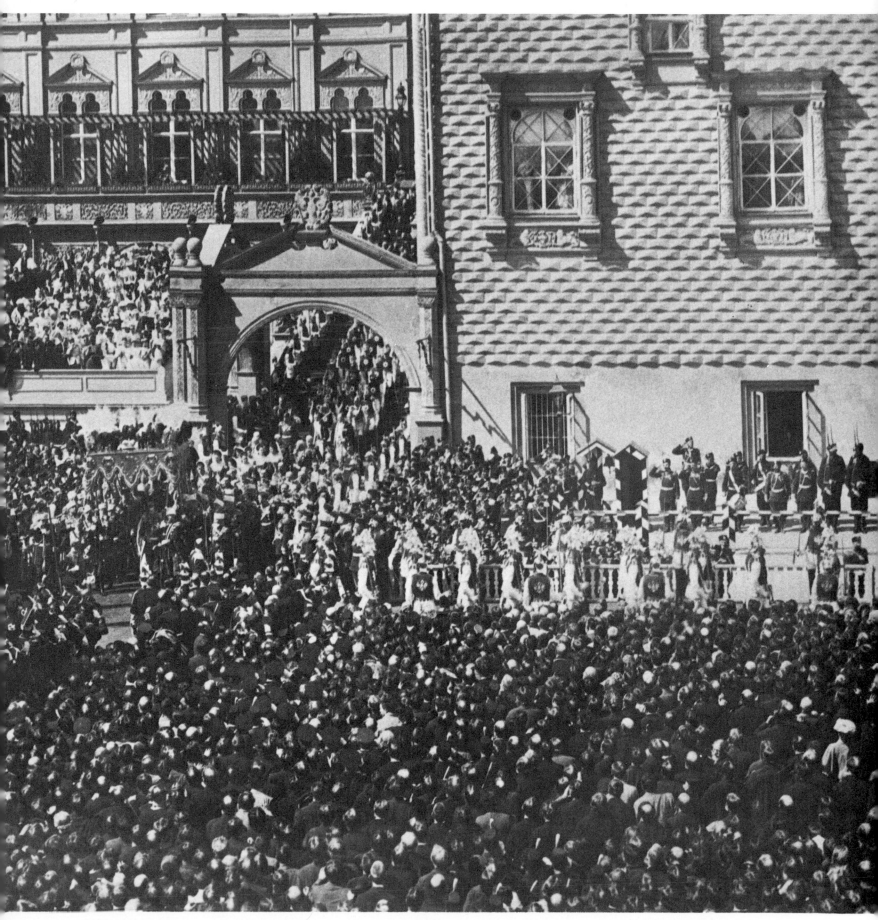

35. "Christmas-tide was aglow with bonfires, the carriages tumbled off the bridges, and the whole funereal city was floating to an unknown destination."

St. Petersburg in 1913.
From *Poem without a Hero,*
by Anna Akhmatova.

35.

A VANISHED WORLD

36, 37. Ladies-in-waiting in court dress. Each wears above her left sleeve a diamond brooch *(shifr)* fashioned after the initial of the imperial family member to whom she is attached.

On February 27, 1903, a costume ball was given by the Emperor in the Winter Palace, at which the guests were dressed in replicas of the costumes of the Russian court and army of the seventeenth century. This was one of the last truly grand social occasions before the Revolution.

38. Mme. Skoropadsky. 39. The Grand Duke Michael Alexandrovich. 40. The Grand Duchess Xenia Alexandrovna. 41. Captain Bezak. 42. Princess Yusupov. 43. General Strukov. 44. Mme. Rodzianko. 45. Count Alexis Musin-Pushkin. 46. Costume ball on a Venetian theme at the Mikhailovsky Palace, c. 1893.

46.

47. Children of the aristocracy dressed in festive "peasant" costumes. The boy wears a coachman's hat topped by peacock feathers. The girl is dressed in a *sarafan* (sleeveless dress) and *kokoshnik* (embroidered headdress). *48, 49. Opposite,* a class in the Imperial School of Ballet, which trained dancers for the Mariinsky (now Kirov) Theater.

50, 52. Russians abroad: a family in Italy, and Prince Menshikov in his troika at Baden-Baden.

51. A children's tea party in Tsarskoye Selo in 1904.

53. The family of Prince and Princess Dolgoruky in St. Petersburg, c. 1897.

54. An officer's family.

55. A room in the Sheremetev Palace at 34 Fontanka, St. Petersburg.

56. Unidentified interior: tea time.

57–60. A room in Alexander Benois's home in St. Petersburg *(58)*, and three unidentified *fin-de-siècle* interiors.

61–68. The Smolny Convent and Institute. The Smolny Convent,
built (1748–62) mainly by Rastrelli and commissioned by the
Empress Elizabeth, is a masterpiece of the Russian Baroque.
Attached to it was the well-known institute founded by Catherine
the Great for the education of young girls of the nobility, c. 1900.

61.

62.

63.

64.

65.

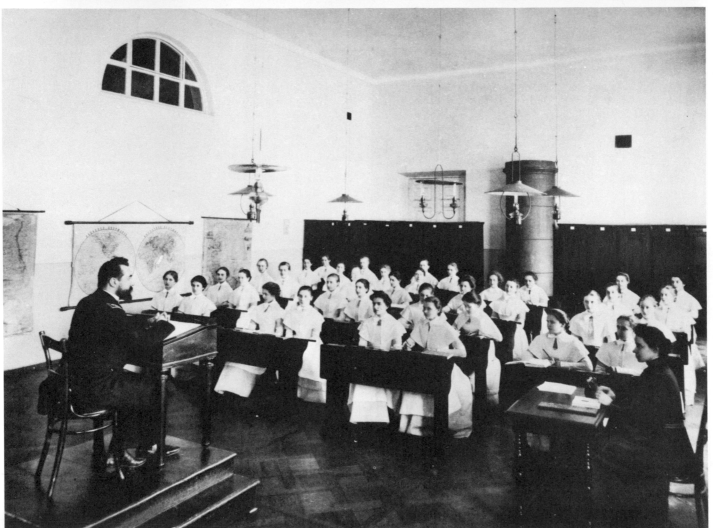

66.

69. The Imperial Corps des Pages, a military school reserved for sons of noblemen and high-ranking officers, educated boys through the university level. It was housed in the Vorontsov Palace in St. Petersburg.

70, 71.   "Pages" of the 1880's.

72. A graduate of the Imperial Law College, c. 1890.

73–76. The Imperial Law College, together with the Corps des Pages and the Alexander Lyceum at Tsarskoye Selo, was one of the most exclusive educational institutions. It formed the cadres for the legal profession, which acquired a growing importance after Alexander II's reforms of 1862–65.

77-80. The Imperial Guard, founded by Peter the Great, had become by the early nineteenth century a first-rate fighting force. *Below,* graduates of the Corps des Pages wearing the uniforms of the regiments of the Guard into which they have been accepted. The three other photographs show officers of the Cavalier Guards at their summer quarters at Krasnoye Selo.

77.

81. Cavalier Guards returning from maneuvers, c. 1908.

82. The University of Saratov on the day of its inauguration, and *(84)* an anatomy class. The university was opened in December 1909; by 1914 there were twelve universities in Russia, most of them founded in the nineteenth century, the oldest being that of Moscow, founded in 1755.

83. Seminarists, their teachers and visitors. St. Petersburg, c. 1900.

85. A class in a technical school, c. 1905.

86. A carpentry class in a provincial primary school.

87. A village school.

88. Schoolchildren in St. Petersburg, c. 1910. Secondary schools in Russia were mainly of two kinds, the *gimnazii* and the *realnye;* the chief difference between them was that the curriculum of the former included the study of classical languages.

90. A grocer's shop in St. Petersburg.

91. A stall in the market of St. Petersburg. Both photographs were taken by William Carrick, c. 1868.

92–96. Carpenters posing for an 1870's photographer, and street types as seen by William Carrick in the 1860's.

97. A tea vendor walks through the market with glasses firmly attached to his waist.

98, 99. Cutting blocks of ice from the frozen Neva, c. 1895, and selling milk from house to house in Moscow.

100. A workers' quarter in one of the poorer districts of St. Petersburg at the close of the century.

101. An old people's home.

102. A children's canteen in St. Petersburg.

103. Food provided by the Red Cross.

104. A hospital ward in a provincial town, c. 1890.

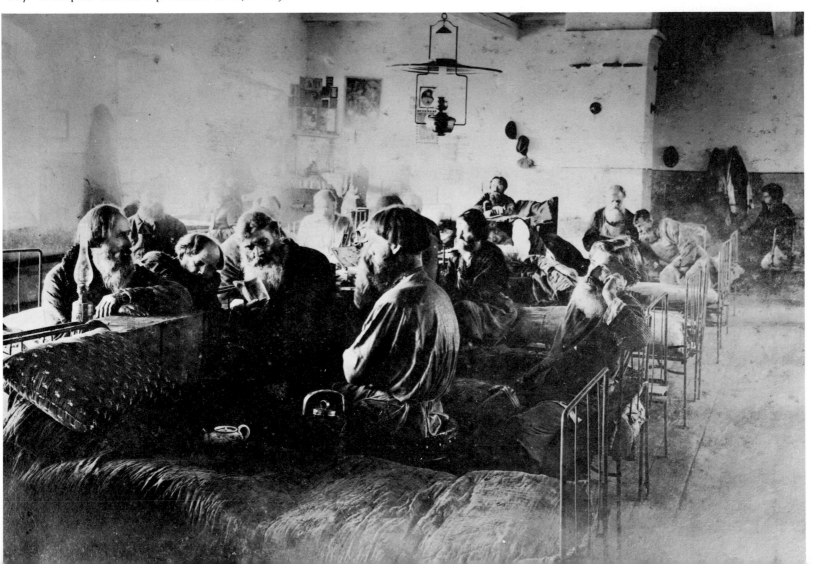

105. Jewish street musicians in the 1890's.

106, 107. Looking at the advertisement for a wild-animal display, and old shoes for sale at the Khitrov market in Moscow. This ill-famed area, where the unemployed mixed with petty criminals and prostitutes, provided the setting for Gorky's play *The Lower Depths*.

108. The Gakental metalwork factory in St. Petersburg, c. 1910.

109. Metalworkers of the 1880's.

110. A vodka distillery in St. Petersburg at the turn of the century.

111. Transporting wood from a sawmill in St. Petersburg, c. 1910.

112. A locomotive factory in the 1890's.

113–115. Three views of the Gakental factory in St. Petersburg, c. 1910.

112.

LIFE ON COUNTRY ESTATES

LIFE ON COUNTRY ESTATES

THE EMANCIPATION OF THE SERFS in 1861 forced the more far-sighted and energetic landowners to develop and modernize the techniques of farming. Though these efforts continued to lag behind the achievements of West European agriculture, the landlords became sellers of grain in the national and international market. Often, however, the new and more rigorous conditions imposed a strain which the more easygoing former serf-owners proved unable to bear, with the result that during the last decades of the nineteenth century much of their land was sold. Between 1877 and 1905 the nobles lost nearly one-third of all their lands, and in the same period the average size of their holdings declined from 1,655 acres to 1,277 acres. Those who retained their property became entrepreneurs of agriculture, while others involved themselves in local administration. Nevertheless the old ways of life died hard, and on the very eve of the First World War this picture of Russian country houses still held good.

At the end of every road, one might still find a "nobleman's nest"—in a house of wood or of plastered brick which would almost certainly present (if it were a building of any size) at least four of those classical columns which had been since the eighteenth century so necessary a part of the stage-setting of manorial life. The house might of course be a small and tumble-down affair, not much better than a peasant's. Or it might be a modest place of a single storey with several thousand volumes in its library, and the walls of the drawing-room over-crowded with eighteenth-century portraits in wig and powder, and nineteenth-century photographs in sideburns and epaulets . . . Or again it might be a more elaborate residence, like that on the 2000-acre domain of the Marshal of Nobility of one of the guberniyas of the steppe . . . Or the house might be one of the country seats of a family of grandees—a huge establishment with exterior walls tinted ochre and white, a columned gateway, a broad forecourt flanked on either side by a colonnade, a columned portico, a rotunda, and a series of apartments furnished in the brass-clawed mahogany of the Napoleonic Empire and the somewhat more humane accoutrements of earlier and later times; with rearwards a formal garden set out with graceless statuary, a great park, and a sweeping view of fields, meadows, white water and wooded hills. [G.T. Robinson, *Rural Russia Under the Old Regime*]

The really grand country houses of the Russian aristocracy were few in number, and most of them, by comparison with the great mansions of Western Europe, were relatively modest in scale and rarely dated back much further than the second half of the eighteenth century. Ostankino, one of the Sheremetev family estates, included a church built in 1668, as well as a private theater. Arkhangelskoye *(overleaf)* was built between the 1780's and the 1830's, at a distance of twenty-three kilometers from Moscow; it belonged to the Yusupov family and housed a particularly fine collection of paintings and objets d'art.

Preceding spread, 116. A luncheon party at Arkhangelskoye. Second on the left, the Grand Duke Sergey Alexandrovich, uncle of the Emperor Nicholas II; his wife, the Grand Duchess Elizabeth (the Empress's sister) wears a dark suit and sits opposite Princess Zinaida Yusupov.

118–120. The main entrance and left wing of Arkhangelskoye, and details of two interiors.

118.

119.

120.

Summer at Arkhangelskoye, c. 1893.

123.

125.

127.

122. Princess Yusupov.

123. Strolling through the village.

124. A game of tennis.

125. A mushroom-picking expedition.

126. Mock fencing.

127. Returning from an afternoon walk.

109

128. The Emperor Alexander III (reclining on the extreme left) with the Empress at a hunt, c. 1888.

Depending on the region, bear, elk, wild boar and wolf were commonly hunted in Russia. Photograph *130* shows a day's trophies, and *131* the midday pause. *Below*, Prince and Princess Yusupov with their sons and a friend after the hunt.

Country estates provided a focus for family life: year after year, scattered members of a family would gather under the same roof, often for long summer months, sharing in a daily routine, inward-looking and timeless. The photographs on these pages record the social role played by the Russian country house.

136. The "Oriental room" in the manor-house of Dikanka, an estate which belonged to the family of Count Kochubey. Dikanka was used by Gogol as the setting for a collection of short stories about the Ukraine.

137. An example of the Russian *style Empire*.

136.

138. A country fair outside the gates of Lysino, a property in the province of Tambov.

139. Count Kochubey with his family in 1903.

137. 138. 139.

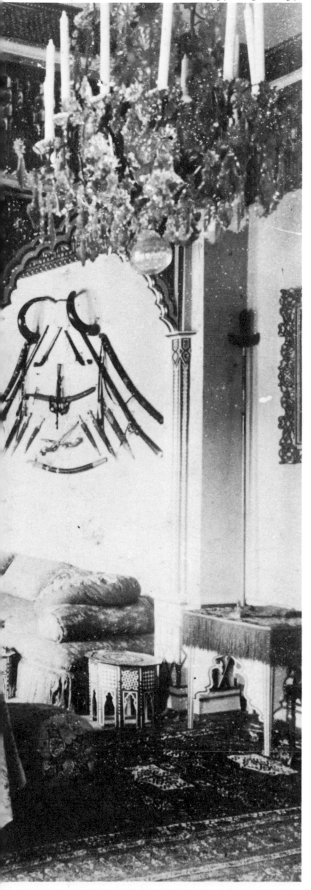

119

143.

144.

145–147. A country house in the Penza province. Its exterior is a
pastiche of traditional peasant styles and follows the
"neo-nationalist" style affected after about 1840; reacting against the
style Empire of the previous generation, architects sought to revive
the traditions of Russian popular art.

148, 149. The drawing room of the Ofrosimov house, c. 1894. Note the Russian nineteenth-century furniture; the tall glazed stove, used universally for heating in Russia; and the walls of unpolished wood, which filled the house with a faint resinous aroma.

151.

150. The *nyanya* (nanny) was a person of central importance in the family household. It was mainly through her influence that, like Pushkin, children heard and learned Russian songs and legends. An archetypal figure, she often strongly resented the coming of foreign governesses and tutors.

151. Count Leo Tolstoy playing patience, surrounded by his family.

152. Countess Tolstoy posing for her daughter and for the sculptor Paul Trubetskoy in Yasnaya Polyana, c. 1894.

153. A game of chess between father and son in the Ossorguine family, sometime after 1900.

Overleaf, 154–157. Prince Evgeny Nikolayevich Trubetskoy with his family in their country home, Beguchino, some twenty-five miles from Kaluga.

152.

153.

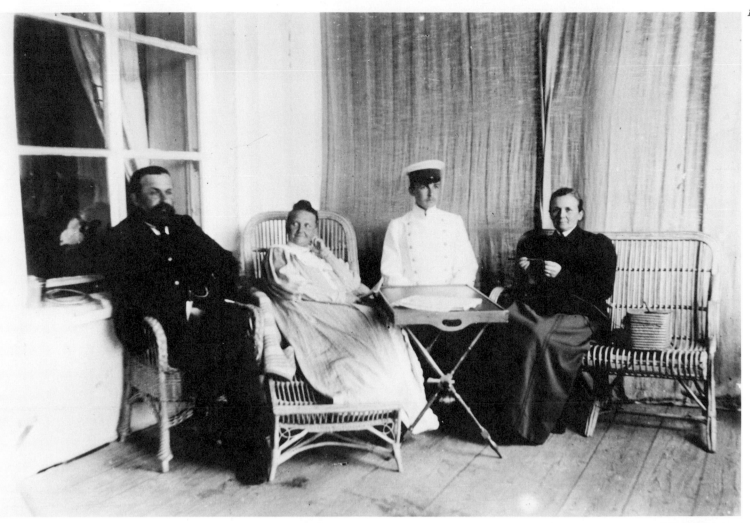

158. The *nyanya*'s bedroom at the Trubetskoy country house.

159. Princess Sophie Trubetskoy with her teacher.

Overleaf:

160. The family of Prince M. I. Kozlovsky, c. 1896. The two sons are flanked by their three teachers: a Frenchman, with the bicycle; a Russian, in a dark suit; and a German.

161. The household servants of a family belonging to the middle gentry, c. 1904.

162. Prince and Princess Shakhovskoy with their servants; the man in the bowler hat is the steward of the estate, and the woman on his right is Prince Shakhovskoy's nurse, an ex-serf liberated in 1861.

163. The household servants of Count I. Uvarov.

164. A *kormilitsa*, or wet-nurse, wearing the characteristic clothes of her profession.

165–167. Traditional jam-making, and nannies with their charges, c. 1895.

Overleaf, 168. A merchant's family round the samovar, c. 1903.

165.

166.

167.

169. Masquerades and amateur theatricals in which neighboring families often participated brought variety to the long months spent away from the city, c. 1898.

170. A visit.

171. Penza: note the photograph of another family house placed above the piano.

172. The back porch of a typical nineteenth-century country house, built in the same style as the one shown in photograph *170.*

Fishing, bathing, mushroom-picking and picnicking were part of the annual summer and autumn ritual. The photographs on these and the next few pages show scenes such as duck-shooting in the Poltava province in the Ukraine *(182)*, hunting with borzoi in Penza *(181)* and the arrival at the village of Yanovo in the Baltic region *(180)*. The borzoi, used for hunting hare and fox as well as wolf, were bred in Russia from the Middle Ages onward and are thought to have been borrowed from the Tatars. Their name means "swift."

173.

180.

181.

184–188. Stewards, gardeners and family retainers. Pilgrims, wandering from shrine to shrine, were widely regarded as "God's people." Tolstoy described them with affection in *Childhood, Boyhood and Youth* and in *War and Peace,* where Princess Mary is portrayed as their friend and protector. The poet Esenin told of how his grandmother's house was often filled with men and women wanderers who sang religious poems descended by word of mouth from the Middle Ages. 186. One of "God's people" resting on the steps of the Trubetskoy country home near Kaluga.

187.

188.

189–192. The happier side of the relations between landowners and peasants. On some estates it was customary for the master or mistress of the house to make gifts on his or her name day; Princess Olga Cantacuzene hands out pieces of material *(190).* Peasants greeting their landlord on Easter Day *(189)*, a peasant wedding in 1908 *(191)* and women and children on Count Baranov's estate *(192).*

189.

190.

191.

192.

195. Village children on a Sunday, c. 1900. The intricate carving on the house and fence in the background was the work of Chinese craftsmen.

196–199. As one moves farther south in European Russia, the woodland gradually diminishes and finally gives way to the open steppe, which before the advent of the plow was covered with feather grass. The steppes of southern Russia, whose wheat nourished the Greek world in antiquity, became in the Middle Ages the home of sheep-rearing, horse-riding nomads from Eurasia who threatened, and in the thirteenth century overwhelmed, the Russian state. Not until the late eighteenth century, when Russia acquired the lands to the north of the Black Sea, did the newly colonized and pacified steppe become once again the granary of Eastern Europe. Its famous "black earth" *(chernozyom)*, rich in humus, is one of the most productive soils in the world.

196. Threshing and hay-making in the 1890's.

196.

200.

201.

The enthusiasm with which some landowners imported agricultural machines from the West (largely from England) sometimes aroused mirth, as did the skepticism with which the peasants regarded these newfangled monsters. "The arrival of these," wrote Mackenzie Wallace, "was an event that was long remembered. The peasants examined them with attention, not unmixed with wonder, but said nothing. When the master explained to them the advantages of the new instruments, they still remained silent. Only one old man, gazing at the threshing machine, remarked in an audible aside, 'A cunning people, these Germans!'"

By the 1890's, generally on private initiative, machinery was being introduced on a number of properties, and the threshing machine *(overleaf, 205 and 207)* was becoming an increasingly common sight.

201. Count and Countess Baranov on their estate at harvest time, c. 1890.

203. The bailiff of a similar property, c. 1900.

Overleaf, 206. A property overseer on the steps of his carriage, custom built to provide sleeping accommodation.

202. 203.

210.

Industrialization continued to spread to the countryside during the first decade of this century. The Trubetskoys and the Kotlyarevskys were among the landowners who made determined efforts to use industrial techniques on their estates. The property of the former *(209)* specialized in livestock; that of the latter *(210–212)* centered on a distillery.

211.

212.

213.

THE VILLAGE

THE VILLAGE

RUSSIAN SOCIETY IN THIS PERIOD remained a predominantly peasant one, and some three-quarters of the empire's population (outside of Finland) earned their living by farming. Life in the Russian village—described, nearly always with sympathy, by the country's writers—was lived much as it had been for centuries past; the peasants' annual cycle of work and prayer, their veneration of the holy man and the pilgrim, and their legends, costumes and folk songs had not changed significantly since the waning of the Middle Ages. Emancipation in 1861 freed them from the personal power of the landowners, but made them dependent on the traditional village commune *(obshchina* or *mir)* for their movement and choice of occupation. The commune now became the basic unit of peasant organization, with collective responsibility for the redistribution of land and, until 1903, for the payment of taxes; the village administration was headed by an elected *starosta,* or village elder. It was not until the legislation of 1906–11, inaugurated by Stolypin, that communal tenure began to give way to private ownership of land by the peasants.

Preceding spread, 213. A village in the mid-1860's near Simbirsk, on the Volga.

214. Peasants at the Kamenka fair, near Simbirsk in 1862. *William Carrick.*

215. 216.

217.

"Yudin village consisted of six small, low-roofed huts which had already begun to lean to one side or the other despite the fact that they had no doubt been put up quite recently . . ." (Turgenev, *The Sportsman's Sketches*, 1852)

The appearance of peasant homes varied greatly in different parts of Russia. In the central and northern areas, where timber was plentiful, they were log-cabins *(izby)*, standing in rows on either side of the village's only thoroughfare. In the Ukraine, by contrast, peasant houses *(khaty)* were usually built of clay and wattle, whitewashed and with thatched roofs. Unlike the northern *izby*, they were arranged in a cluster.

216. An *izba* of the Middle Volga area, c. 1870. *William Carrick.*

217. A village near Borispol in the region of Kiev, in the Ukraine.

218-221. Peasant buildings in the far north: a village near Lake Onega. The timber houses of northern Russia often comprised two stories, whereas the *izba* generally consisted of a main room, a cellar and a loft. In both, however, the large brick stove—second in importance only to the "beautiful corner" reserved for family icons —was used for heating, cooking, baking bread and, last but not least, for sleeping.

The traditionally large peasant family, often represented by three generations living together under the authority of the head of the house, began to disintegrate after the Emancipation Decree of 1861.

218.

219. 220. 221.

222.

222. Interior of a Ukrainian *khata*, its walls covered with icons.

223. The main room of an *izba*.

224. A family grouped together in one room; note the woman sleeping on the stove.

225.

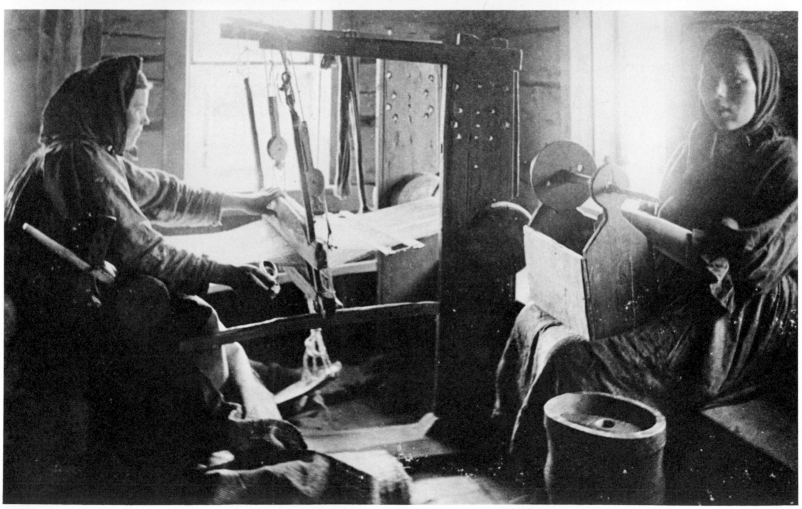

226.

225. Peasants from the Middle Volga area, c. 1885.

226, 227. Women at the loom.

228. Simbirsk, c. 1865. *William Carrick.*

229, 230. Cottage industry: spinning, weaving, carving of wooden house utensils, block-printing and basket-weaving. These were usually part-time occupations during the winter months, bringing in a much needed income. In the late nineteenth century, however, home industry began to be stifled by the growth of large factories, c. 1890.

231–233. Peasants on the way to the Kamenka fair, in the Simbirsk region, and waiting for the ferry on the banks of the Sura, c. 1870. The normal dress of a peasant consisted of a long shirt, held at the waist by a belt and worn over baggy trousers, which were tucked into leggings, and a rough woolen or sheepskin coat in the winter. On Sundays and other holidays, he sometimes wore a dark-blue double-breasted coat. Bast shoes *(lapti)*, made of plaited birch bark, were replaced, in the case of more prosperous peasants, by leather boots. Felt boots *(valenki)* were worn only in the winter.
William Carrick.

231.

234.

234, 235. Religious processions on great feasts, saints' days and major seasonal events were usually marked by the carrying of an icon of the Virgin around the village or through the fields by clergy and lay people, c. 1900.

236.

236. Borispol, a Ukrainian village near Kiev, c. 1880.

237. Building a barn near Borispol in the 1870's. *Below*, farm hands during a meal. The photograph was taken in the region of Simbirsk in the 1860's.

239.   237.

238. Plowing with the traditional wooden plow *(sokha)*, which by the turn of the century was rapidly giving way to the iron plow of the West European type. *Below*, a farmer with his son and two hired laborers, c. 1880.

238.

240.

With a wife and family to support, the village priest often led a life little different from that of his parishioners. The married clergy, debarred from the highest ranks in the church administration—which were reserved for monks—tended to form a separate caste.

242. Elders *(starosty),* or elected leaders of the village community, wearing bronze medals as the insignia of their office.

243. A volost court in session. From the late eighteenth century until the Revolution, the volost court was a basic unit of village administration. Extended to former serfs by the Emancipation Decree of 1861, these courts dealt with cases involving disputes between peasants.

244. A volost assembly. The meetings were held in the open air, primarily because of the absence of a building large enough to contain all the members (the church was reserved for religious purposes only). Assemblies usually took place on a Sunday or a holiday, when there was ample leisure.

245. The village fire brigade.

246. The steam-bath house *(banya),* which dates back to the Middle Ages, was a national institution, c. 1890.

247. Religious ceremonies and fairs broke the monotony of daily life, attracting a motley crowd of tradesmen, pilgrims and wandering minstrels.

248. A priest and his wife on a Sunday visit to a neighboring landowner's home.

249. "Out of the depths have I cried unto thee, O Lord."

MONKS AND PILGRIMS

MONKS AND PILGRIMS

ONASTERIES WERE A FOCUS of religious life in Russia since the country's conversion to Christianity in the tenth century. They attracted men and women in search of the spiritual life and were the breeding ground for members of the higher clergy. Their location often testified to their founders' sense of natural beauty.

One of the oldest and most revered was the Monastery of the Caves (Pechersky) in Kiev, founded in the eleventh century on a hill overlooking the Dnieper (*preceding spread*). The monastery church is the Cathedral of the Dormition, one of the major churches of medieval Russia; it was decorated by artists from Byzantium in 1083–89. Beneath, in gallery after gallery hewn out of rock, lie the bodies of holy hermits who from the earliest days of the monastery lived and died within its walls.

251. Wanderer, c. 1870. These "people of God" included men who collected alms for the building of churches and itinerant bards who sang or recited religious poems whose origins lay deep in Russia's past. A striking feature of Russia's religious life, which stemmed from the Middle Ages and survived even the 1917 Revolution, were the pilgrims who walked from shrine to shrine within the country or journeyed to distant holy places, such as Palestine or Mount Athos. The Church housed them in special hostels and blessed them as they set out on their way.

252. The vestment worn over this monk's habit, depicting the instruments of Christ's passion and inscribed with a text from the Gospel of St. Luke, shows that he is a hermit who has taken the strictest of monastic vows (the "Great Skhima"), c. 1870.

253. In the nineteenth century a notable center of religious life was the Hermitage of Optino, in the province of Kaluga in central Russia. A group of outstanding *startsy,* or teachers of the spiritual life, became friends or mentors of Russian intellectuals. The best known of these hermits, Father Amvrosy, gave personal guidance to many prominent writers of the second half of the century, including Dostoyevsky and Tolstoy. The *starets* Zosima in *The Brothers Karamazov* was partly modeled on him.

254. The entrance to the courtyard of a monastery, c. 1885.

255.

256.

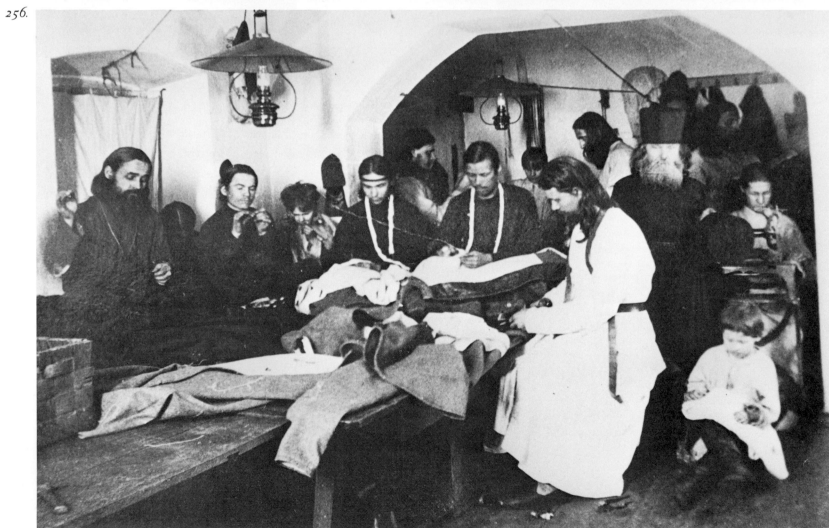

255–258. Preparing a meal, bookbinding, clothes-making and icon-painting: everyday activities at the Monastery of Valamo on Lake Ladoga, founded in the early fifteenth century.

259–261. Pilgrims and wanderers.

262.

262. Blind wandering pilgrims, c. 1870.

263, 264. Russian pilgrims in Jerusalem, c. 1898.

RIVERS AND TOWNS

RIVERS AND TOWNS

THE RIVERS OF RUSSIA, with their meandering courses and far-flung basins, form a network of waterways unique in Europe. From the dawn of Russian history they have provided areas of settlement, commercial or strategic sites for the growth of towns and routes of communication inside the country and with the surrounding world. With the extension of steam water transport, the rivers provided a service to Russian industry, which developed rapidly in the early 1870's, that was crucial until the advent of railways at the end of the nineteenth century. Opening this section is a photograph (266) of the Dnieper in the preindustrial age; it was taken near Kiev in 1852 by Roger Fenton, who in that year is said to have accompanied Sir Charles Vignoles, commissioned by Emperor Nicholas I to build a bridge across the river.

By the 1890's the industrial boom of the early 1870's had led to the expansion of the metallurgical industry, which was also stimulated by the program of railway building during that decade; large metallurgical plants were created in the Ukraine, based on the coal mines of the Donets region, in Yekaterinoslav on the Dnieper and on Krivoy Rog farther west. A second result of the boom was the further development of the more traditional Russian textile industry. The latter had its roots in the art of cotton spinning and weaving, which until about 1825 scarcely rose above the level of cottage industry. By the second half of the century, however, cotton manufacture had become the country's largest single industrial asset. Its main centers were the provinces of Moscow, Vladimir and Lodz in Russian Poland (the former two enjoyed the advantage of easy access by river to the cotton-producing areas of Central Asia). A new class of industrialists emerged, some of them first- or second-generation descendants of serfs. The town of Ivanovo-Voznesensk, north of Vladimir, was founded on one of Count Sheremetev's estates, and by the end of the century had become the second largest center of the Russian cotton industry.

The extent of this industrial boom can be gauged by the fact that between 1890 and 1900 the output of coal in southern Russia increased nearly fourfold, while in the empire as a whole the production of cotton thread doubled. The photographs on the following pages illustrate a number of industrial enterprises in the Russia of this time.

267. Peasants of the Simbirsk region, c. 1865.

269, 270. Two commercial towns on the upper and lower Volga in the 1890's: Rybinsk, near Yaroslavl, dealing in grain and caviar, and Tsaritsyn (later Stalingrad, now Volgograd), trading in timber, grain and fish.

268. Bridge-building in 1870.

268.

271.

271–273. A factory, administered by the Metallurgical Society of Southern Russia, under construction in the Dnieper region in 1887.

272.

Overleaf, 274. A blast furnace in central Russia, c. 1890.

273.

73246

275. View of the main part of the steel, sheet and tin-plate mill as completed in 1907.

276. The Lysva steel mill in the Ural Mountains, near Perm. In 1899 the proprietor of this district, Count P. P. Shuvalov, mortgaged the area—some one and a half million acres of mineral lands and forest—for the purpose of erecting a modern steel mill.

277. The management and visitors from St. Petersburg.

275.

278. The Alexandrovsky factory near Yekaterinoslav: general view of the blast furnace and coke ovens, 1889–90.

279. The religious ceremony at the laying of the cornerstone for the bar mill at Lysva, c. 1898.

280, 281. The plate rolling mill at the Sormovo Works, founded in 1849, on the Volga near Nizhny-Novgorod, c. 1897.

278.

279. 280. 281.

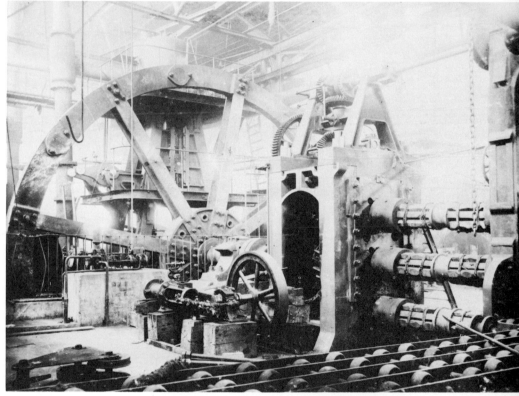

The Sysert factory, located in the Urals about fifty kilometers from Yekaterinburg, was founded in 1732. The Seversky factory was one of five comprising the complex. Its privately owned mines produced iron, copper, chrome and gold.

282–284. Three views of the Seversky factory showing the blast furnace, the steel mill and the water conduit pipes, c. 1896.

285.

286.

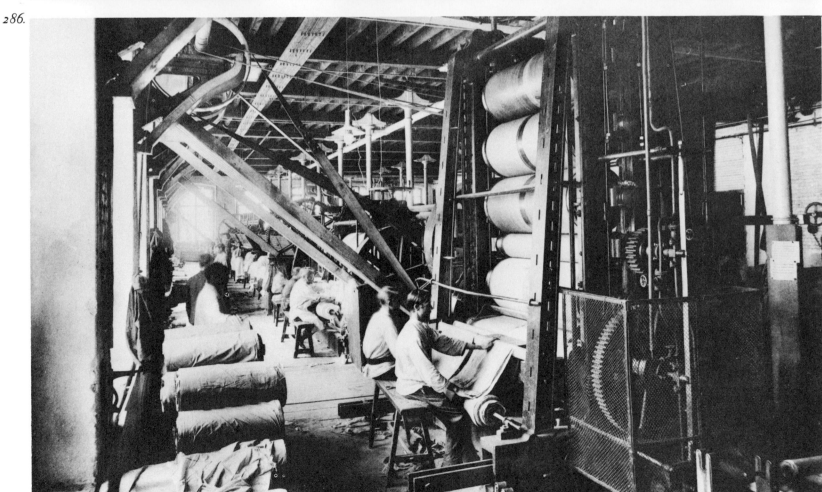

285–288. The Konovalov textile enterprises in Bonyachki, near Kineshma on the Volga, in the province of Kostroma, were founded in the early nineteenth century. In its technical equipment and welfare facilities for workers, the factory was a model industrial complex, c. 1910.

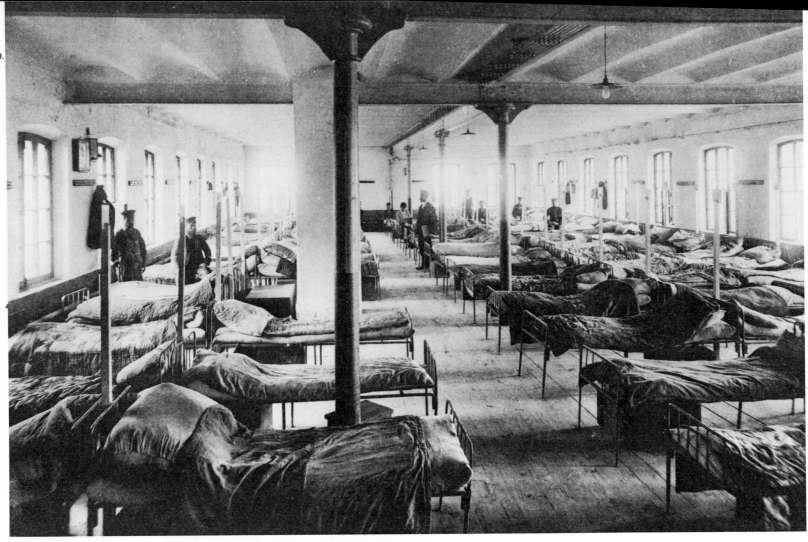

The Konovalov enterprises: the workmen's dormitory *(289)*, the dining room in the quarters built for retired workers *(290)*, and the room of a married working couple, c. 1910 *(291)*.

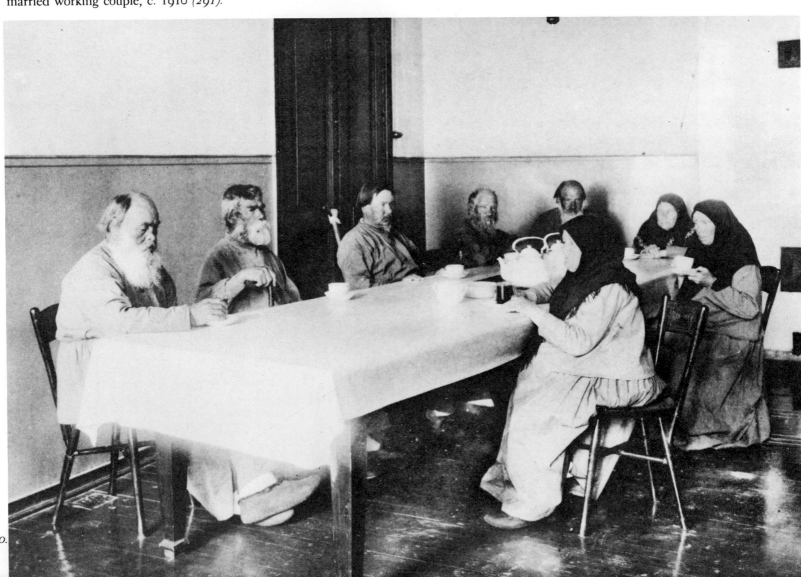

292. Wooden bunks in the workmen's dormitory of an unidentified factory, c. 1900.

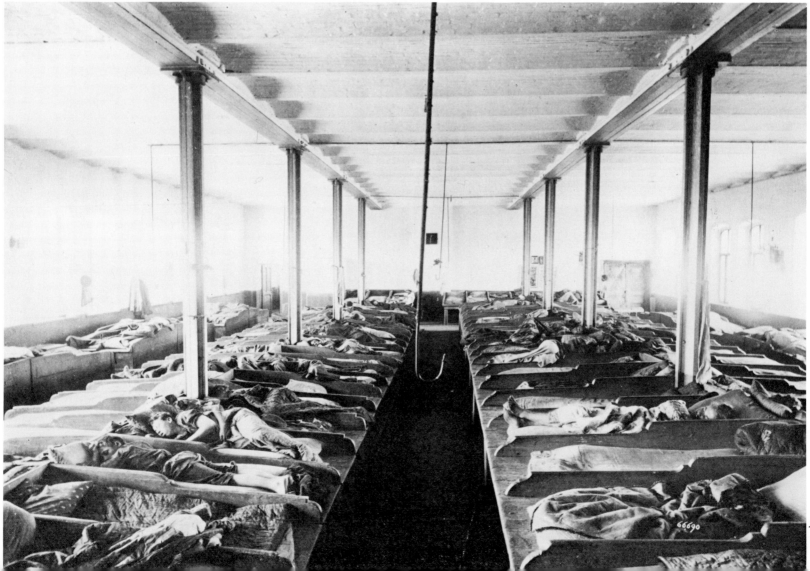

Shoe industry at the turn of the century. Founded in 1860, this factory in the eastern part of European Russia was initially a modest family enterprise; by 1900 it had developed into one of the country's main boot-manufacturing centers, and during World War I it produced three thousand pairs of boots per day.

A general view of the factory (296) and of the main street of the town in which it was situated (293); the proprietor's family in their garden (295) and youthful guards at an entrance to the factory (294).

Overleaf, 297–300. The processing of leather and felt, the latter used to make *valenki*, a weatherproof type of boot worn in Russia during the winter.

301. Nizhny-Novgorod (now Gorky), on the confluence of the Volga and the Oka—a point of great commercial and strategic importance—dominated the river routes which led to central Russia, the Urals and Siberia, and down the Volga to the Caspian Sea, Transcaucasia and Iran. Since its foundation in the thirteenth century it played a major role in Russian history, acting as a forward base for the conquest by Muscovy of the land of the Volga Tatars. It was in 1559, with the capture of Astrakhan by Ivan the Terrible, that the whole of the Volga came under Russian control.

The city's commercial importance was enhanced by its famous summer fair, founded on a nearby site in 1525. In 1817 it was transferred to its present location on the left bank of the Oka. The largest of all Russian fairs, it provided a commercial link between the center of the country and the Urals, Siberia, Transcaucasia, and with the neighboring lands of Persia, India, Afghanistan and China. Furs, leather, metalwork, wheat, fish, tea, timber and textiles were among the products sold at the Nizhny-Novgorod fair.

301.

302. Workmen of a Volga steamship company, c. 1890.

303, 304. The Volga at Yaroslavl and at Nizhny-Novgorod, c. 1900.

305. Peasants and boatmen of Nizhny-Novgorod.

Nizhny-Novgorod during fair time *(307)*, a peasant merchant in 1885 *(306)* and the bell market *(308)*.

309. A photograph of Kiev taken in 1852 by Fenton. The church of St. Sophia in the background was built in the eleventh century, decorated with Byzantine mosaics, and served as the cathedral of Kiev, Russia's first capital and the "mother of the Russian cities."

310. Kharkov, in the Ukraine, a university town and the
administrative center of the iron industry in southern Russia, as seen
in 1870. It was a large provincial town with a main square, at the
center of which stood the characteristically low-roofed shops.

310.

311, 312. Street scenes in Nizhny-Novgorod, c. 1890. The photographs
on these and the following pages detail the presence of the church
in provincial public life.

313.

314.

317. Tatars from Kazan, c. 1885. The Tatars of the Middle Volga were descended from the inhabitants of the Khanate of Kazan, which was conquered and annexed to Russia by Ivan IV in 1552. The Khanate was a successor-state of the Golden Horde, whose rulers were the overlords of most of Russia from 1240 to 1480. The Volga Tatars, Muslim and Turkic-speaking, had acquired by the turn of the nineteenth century a prosperous merchant class and an intelligentsia, attracted by Western ideas of democracy and nationalism.

318. A Tatar mosque near Simbirsk, c. 1868.

319. Tatars from Kazan.

320. The market in Ufa. Founded by the Russians in the second half of the sixteenth century to forward the colonization of the land of the Bashkirs, a Turkic Muslim people, Ufa was by 1900 a center of trade for the Urals region, as well as an important mining town, c. 1885.

321. Inside a Kalmyk *yurta*. The Kalmyks, a race of horse-riding seminomadic pastoralists, lived west of the lower Volga and along the northern and western shores of the Caspian Sea. Buddhist by religion, they speak a Mongolian language and live for the most part in traditional *yurta*, a conical tentlike structure whose framework of wooden lattice is covered with birch or felt. The place of honor is opposite the door, just beyond the hearth.

322. A Bashkir musician, c. 1900.

323. Kirgiz musicians in Orenburg in 1900.

320.

From time immemorial the middle Volga area was the home of Finnic peoples, who began to merge with the Slav colonists in the early Middle Ages. Long after their incorporation into the Muscovite realm and their formal conversion to Christianity, many retained their ancestral pagan or shamanistic customs. They included the Finno-Ugrian Mordva between the middle Volga and the Oka, the linguistically related Cheremis north of the middle Volga and, still farther north, as far as the basin of the Pechora, the Zyrians or Komi.

324. A young bull about to be sacrificed by the Cheremis, c. 1900.

324.

325. Russian and Samoyed pilots bound for the mouth of the Pechora. The Samoyeds or Nentsy lived mainly in the tundra between the White Sea and the lower Yenisey, and in the period covered in this book were reindeer pastoralists, hunters and fishermen who maintained their shamanistic traditions.

326. A Zyrian family, c. 1890.

327. Fishing in the Urals.

325.

328, 329. Orenburg Cossacks. The Cossacks, whose name derives from a Turkic word, *kazak*, meaning adventurer or rebel, were frontiersmen who, at least in the Ukraine, were often peasants whose ancestors had fled their landlords. The term came to be applied to similar communities of soldier-farmers settled on the borderlands of Russia, which were expected to defend, and later to extend, the frontiers of the empire. Their military qualities and their adventurous and democratic—not to say anarchic—social proclivities made them a favorite subject for romantically inclined writers. By 1900 there were twelve Cossack armies stationed on or near the borders; the Orenburg *voysko*, under its own *ataman*, numbered 530,000 men.

330. Orenburg in 1880. Founded on the boundary of European and Asian Russia in the first half of the eighteenth century, the fortress of Orenburg became a military and administrative center for the Russian control of the Trans-Volga region, and played an important role in Russia's trade with Central Asia.

The rich mining district of the Urals was exploited on a large scale by Peter the Great, who created an iron industry which in the middle of the eighteenth century led the whole of Europe. Later, however, and especially after 1861, the metallurgical industry of this region declined sharply, though in 1913 the Urals were, after the Ukraine, the second most important pig-iron-producing region in the empire. The photographs on these and the next two pages show gold mining in the Urals in 1867.

332. 333.

SIBERIA

SIBERIA

EYOND THE URALS, in the vast area bounded by the Arctic and the Pacific oceans and in the south by Kazakhstan, Mongolia and China, lies Siberia. Much of the country is covered by the great forest belt (the *taiga*), which in the north merges into the Arctic tundra, where dwarf bushes, lichen and moss grow precariously on a permafrost soil.

The Russian conquest of Siberia began in 1581–82, when a small band of Cossacks commanded by Yermak, a mercenary of the Stroganov family from the western Urals, subjugated the Tatar Khanate of western Siberia. Henceforth, along the tributaries of the majestic Siberian rivers—the Ob, the Yenisey and the Lena—and from one stockaded post to another, the conquest continued without hindrance, and in 1649 the Russians reached Okhotsk on the Pacific coast. The aboriginal tribes—Turkic, Finno-Ugrian and Mongol—offered no effective resistance and sometimes intermarried with their conquerors. The imperial government used Siberia as a place of banishment and hard labor, while in the 1890's and again after 1904 peasants were encouraged by state subsidies and other privileges to settle there. Siberia's economic importance was enhanced by the discovery of

rich deposits of gold, silver, iron, copper, lead and salt, which led to the growth of local industries, and by the construction between 1891 and 1905 of the Trans-Siberian Railway, which linked Moscow and Vladivostok on a journey lasting ten days.

Before the arrival of Russian colonists in the mid-seventeenth century, Siberia was inhabited by a large number of small ethnic groups whose culture was adapted to the natural environment. In the south were pastoral nomads tending herds of sheep and horses. In the middle forest zone lived hunters and food-gatherers. The northern tundra was home to nomads with herds of domestic reindeer. In the far north the shores of the Arctic Ocean were settled by maritime hunters of seal, walrus and whale. These groups spoke different languages, the most important being Finno-Ugric (Ostyaks and Voguls), Altaic (Buryat) and Turkic (Yakut). Except perhaps for the Yakut, these peoples were primitive and loosely organized. Their religion focused on the figure of the shaman, the defender and healer of the community and the mediator between the natural and the spiritual worlds.

Preceding spread, 338. On the Kolyma River.

339A, 339B. Two ways of traveling in Siberia: the traditional horse-drawn *kibitka* and, ridden by a Yakut, the reindeer.

340–342. Ostyaks of the Ob and their fishing boats. Like the Tungus and the Voguls, the Ostyaks of western Siberia were primarily hunters and fishermen. The Tungus, who lived partly between the Ob and the Yenisey and partly in eastern Siberia, are shown in photograph 346 (overleaf). The other three photographs are of a camp of reindeer hunters in the *taiga* (343), a Christian grave in the forest (344) and a hunting party riding Bactrian camels (345).

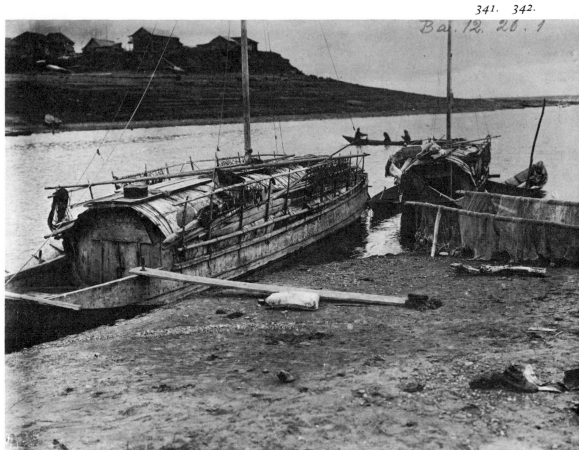

Ba. 12. 26. 1

341. 342.

347. The inauguration of a bridge on the Trans-Siberian Railway. In the 1890's a series of famines in European Russia, together with the construction of this railway, prompted the government policy of encouraging free peasant settlement in Siberia. Here settlers are shown in a temporary camp near Achinsk, between Tomsk and Krasnoyarsk (350), and receiving a meal at public expense (348).

349. A Siberian family, presumably of mixed descent.

347.

348. 349. 350.

351–354. Russian settlers in Siberia at the end of the century.

355–358. The many tributaries and easy portages of the Ob, the Yenisey and the Lena—the great north-flowing rivers of Siberia—enabled the early fur traders to cross the country with amazing speed; and until the completion of the railway, they provided the only effective routes of west–east transportation.

357. Russian settlers traveling on the Ob.

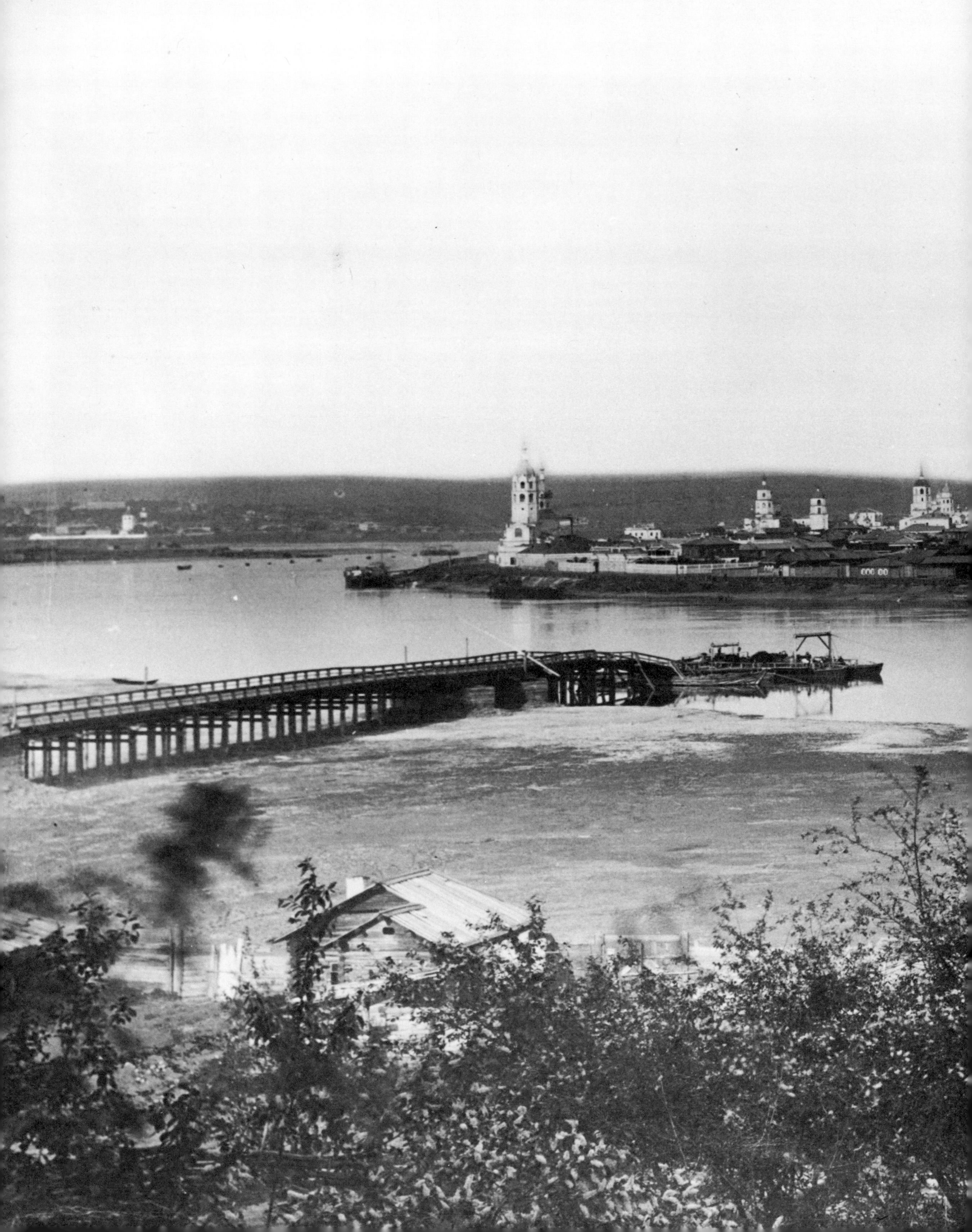

359. Irkutsk in 1890, a few years before the coming of the railway. Founded in 1652 on the right bank of the Angara, near Lake Baikal, Irkutsk was in the nineteenth century the administrative capital of eastern Siberia and the major industrial center of the country. The thousand-mile journey which exiles made on foot to Irkutsk was said to last three months. Siberia, a place of exile for criminals since 1648, became a land of banishment for political prisoners in 1729.

In 1891 it was estimated that there were in exile in Siberia 100,000 Polish rebels, 40,000 Russian criminals, 50,000 Russian political exiles and 5,000 wives who had chosen to follow their husbands.

360. A woman arriving at her place of exile.

362. A convicts' barge.

361. Political exiles, c. 1900.

363. Prisoners convicted of criminal offenses working on the railroad.

364, 366, 367. Political exiles in Siberia in the 1890's.

365. An abandoned salt mine, used as a church, in Viluysk.

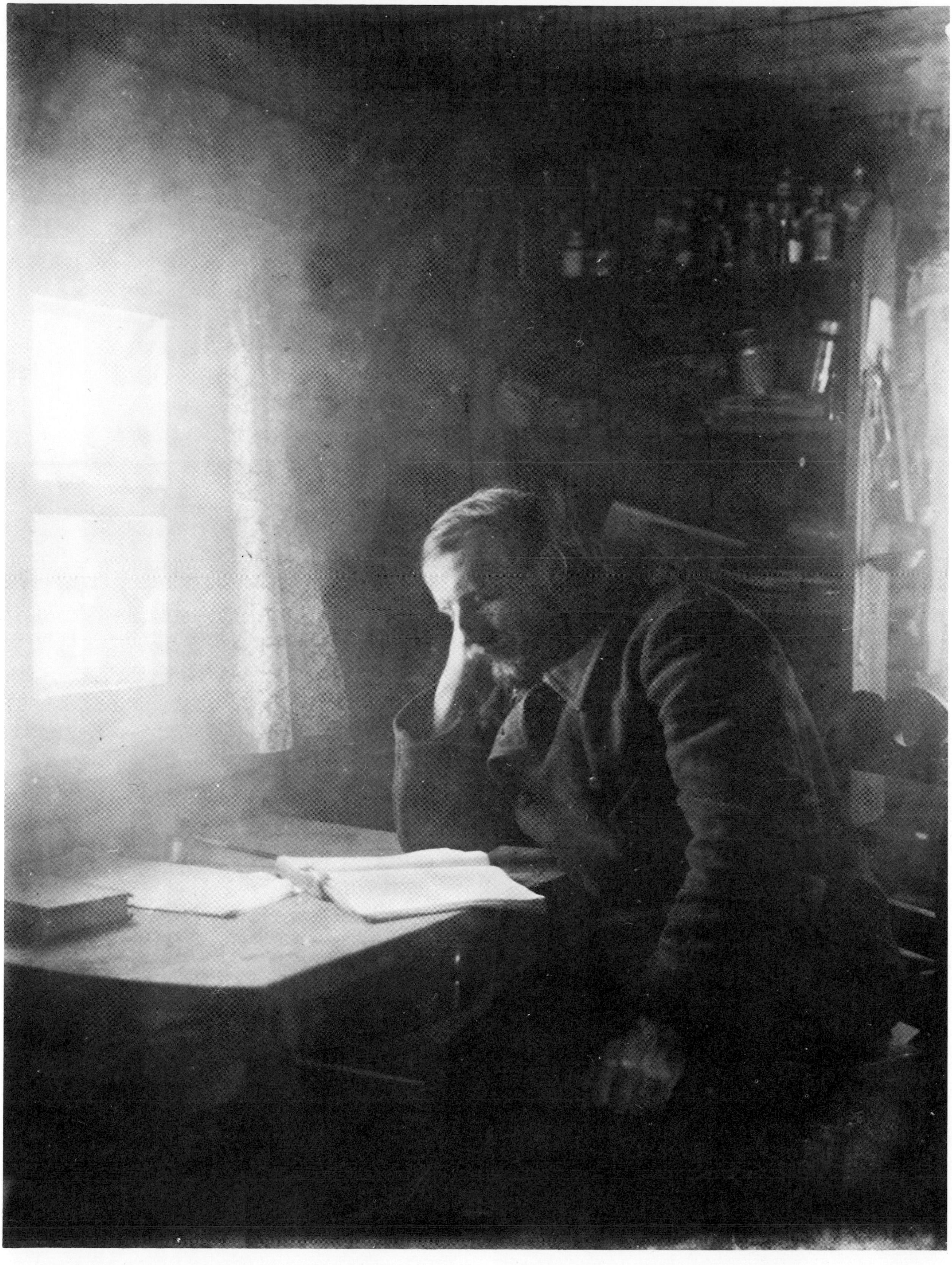

The Alexandrovsky Central Prison near Irkutsk: a workshop in the hard-labor prison *(368)* and the convicts' barracks *(369)*.

370, 371. Prison interiors in Siberia, c. 1900.

372.

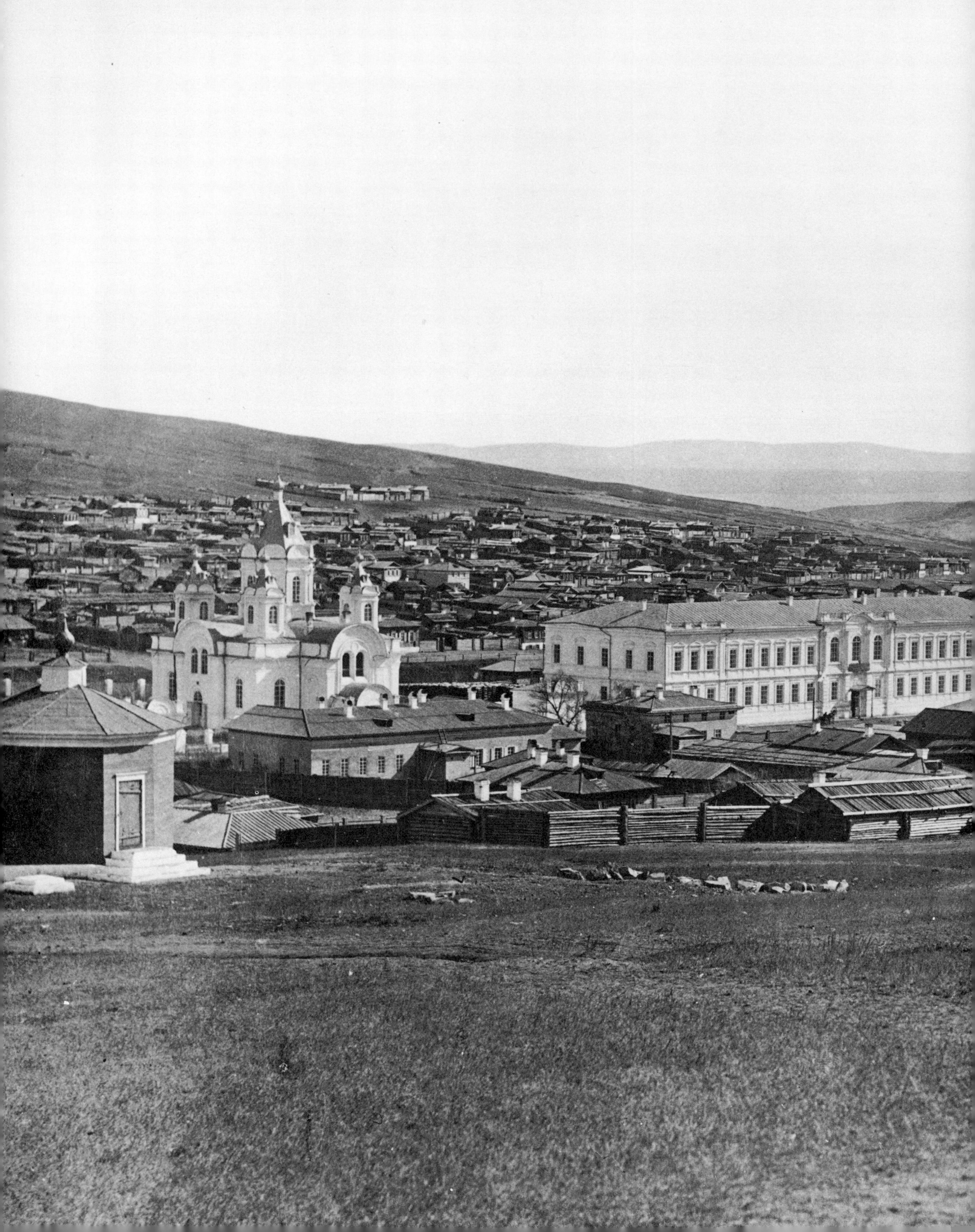

372. Troitskosavsk, in the Trans-Baikal region, near Kyakhta, lay a few miles from the Chinese border. The town was founded in 1727.

373. Chinese workers at a graphite mine founded in 1844. This early daguerreotype was taken by J. P. Alibert, a French fur trader who discovered graphite in the Tunkisk Mountains west of Irkutsk and for whom this mine was named. The graphite, of particularly fine quality, was used by Faber for its pencils.

The Buryats, a Mongol people living to the south and east of Lake Baikal, were gradually absorbed into the empire in the course of the seventeenth century, while the Russians, who built the towns and organized the local industries, lived a colonial existence alongside the local communities. The Buryat religion, in the indigenous tradition of Siberian tribes, combined Buddhism with shamanism, the shaman being both priest and medicine man, curing sickness and directing sacrifices.

374. A Buryat family, c. 1890. The women wear earrings and medallions inscribed with Tibetan prayers.

375, 376. A Buddhist ritual chariot and, *below,* a Soyot (or Tuvan) shaman in action, c. 1900.

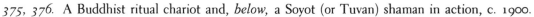

377.

377. A wealthy Yakut household. The Yakut, one of the most advanced Siberian peoples, were expert potters and ironworkers who lived mainly in the basin of the middle Lena. By the mid-eighteenth century many of them had been baptized, and in the nineteenth, all were officially "registered" as Orthodox.

378. Fur-trading Yakut leaving for the fair in the traditional sleigh.

378.

379. Blacksmiths.

380. Interior of a Yakut house.

381–383. The Kachin were a Turkic-speaking tribe dwelling in the steppe on the left bank of the Upper Yenisey. The matchmaker (381) wears the festive hat made of fox fur. Bride-stealing was part of the Kachin marriage ritual.

The Amur, one of the largest rivers of Asiatic Russia, was explored by Russian Cossacks in 1644. In 1858 it was agreed that, from its junction with the Argun to the sea, it should form the boundary between the Russian and Chinese empires. Two years later, by the Treaty of Peking, the land east and south of the lower Amur down to Vladivostok was added to the Russian Empire.

The lower Amur region *(384)*, traveling Japanese acrobats *(385)*, Cossacks of Mariinsky Post *(386)* and merchants on the Amur in the region of the Khingan Mountains *(387)*.

388–390. The offshore island of Sakhalin, at the southern entrance to the Sea of Okhotsk, was declared a joint Russian-Japanese possession in 1855. Between 1875, when the whole island was acquired by the Russians, and 1905, when the southern part reverted to Japan, Sakhalin was used as a vast penal colony. The native inhabitants were the Ainu, who spoke a language unrelated to any other known tongue and whose religion centered on the forces of nature and the cult of ancestors; ritual sacrifice of bear was a prominent feature.

391. Nikolayevsk, founded in 1850 on the estuary of the Amur, opposite Sakhalin, c. 1880.

389.

391.

390.

392–394. Convicts of Siberia and Sakhalin. Chekhov, who visited the island in the early 1890's, exposed the inhuman treatment of the convicts in *Island of Sakhalin*, published in 1894. In 1900, according to official statistics, Sakhalin contained 3,000 exiled peasants, 7,500 exiled settlers and 7,000 convicts.

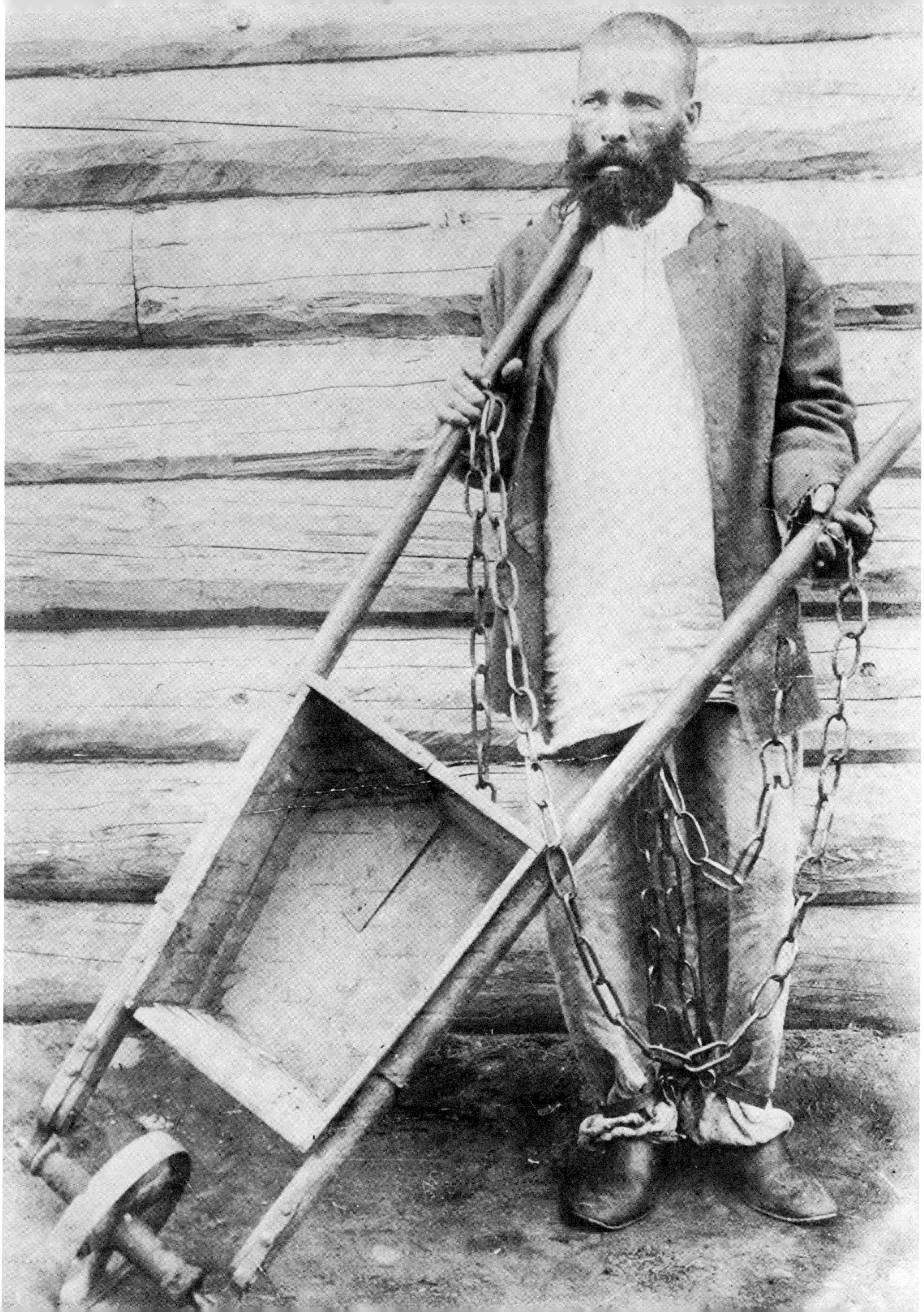

394.

395. A new Russian settlement in Kirgizia in the 1890's. The Kirgiz, Turkic-speaking and Muslim, were in this period mainly nomadic cattle, horse and camel breeders. Their home, predominantly mountainous, comprised the great Eurasian steppe which extended from the Carpathian Mountains to Mongolia and was one of the major highways of migration and invasion in the history of the world; it also included the western part of the Tien Shan range, on the borders of Sinkiang, and the fertile Fergana Valley. Kirgizia was annexed to the Russian Empire in the second half of the nineteenth century.

396–399. Kirgiz, c. 1900.

400–402. A Kirgiz family in festive dress, and Kirgiz elders, c. 1890.

TURKESTAN

404.

TURKESTAN

RUSSIAN TURKESTAN WAS A TERM formerly applied to the area of Central Asia between Siberia in the north, Afghanistan, Tibet and India in the south, the Caspian in the west, and Mongolia in the east. In this land of ancient civilization, inhabited by Turkic peoples—Uzbek, Turcoman, Kazakh and Kirgiz—the Russians established colonies and protectorates in the 1860's and 1870's. The principal stages in this colonial expansion were the capture of Tashkent, which became the center of Russian power in Central Asia, and of Samarkand; the acceptance of the Khans of Khiva and Bukhara of a Russian protectorate and the annexation of the Khanate of Kokand. This enabled the Russians to gain access to the raw cotton produced in the region, which by 1890 provided nearly a quarter of the needs of the Russian textile industry.

In 1881, as a result of the conquest of the Turcomans between the Aral and Caspian seas, a new Trans-Caspian province of the Russian Empire was established under the governor-general of the Caucasus. In the same year, construction began on the Trans-Caspian Railway, which was to link the eastern shores of the Caspian with the empire's new Central Asian possessions. The railway reached the Amu-Darya in 1886.

Preceding spread, 403. The Fortress of Chardzhou near Bukhara, on the Amu-Darya River, c. 1880.

404. Turkestan merchants.

Overleaf:

405. The Emir of Chardzhou.

406. Turcoman notables in Merv, c. 1890.

407. Scribes and accountants in the palace of the Emir of Chardzhou.

Bukhara, an important commercial center, the capital of an emirate and long regarded as the holy city of Central Asia, became a Russian protectorate in 1873. In 1914, according to Baedecker, the city contained 360 mosques and 109 theological schools. The Kalyan Mosque *(409)* was built in 1121–22 and restored in the fifteenth century. Bukhara was the meeting place for Persians, Indians, Armenians, Tatars, Kirgiz, Turcomans, Uzbeks, Tadzhiks and Jews (whose ancient community played an important role in the city's life).

408. Russian officers and officials visiting the Khan of Merv in 1887. The young Khan (in Russian uniform) stands on the far left, while his mother sits in the center.

410. The caravan halting place in Merv, 1890.

411. Russian officers on a visit to Urgut, near Samarkand, in 1887.

412. Bukhara: The mausoleum of the Samanids.

413, 414. The synagogue and the Jewish school in Bukhara, c. 1887.

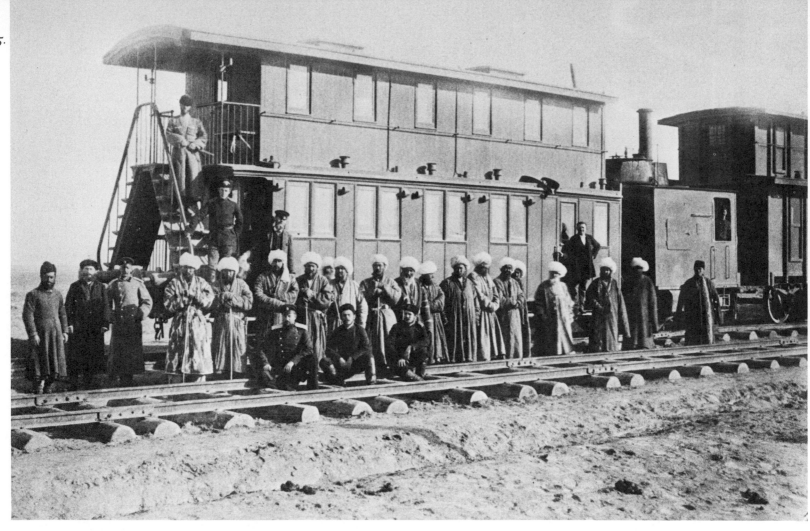

415, 417. The first railway engine to cross the Amu-Darya in 1886.

416. A group of traveling players.

416.

418. Beggars of Khiva.

419.

THE CAUCASUS
AND THE CRIMEA

THE CAUCASUS AND THE CRIMEA

THE PROVERBIAL MELTING POT of the Caucasus, said to exceed fifty peoples, had long been the object of Russia's imperialistic designs. Georgia was annexed in 1801, and northern Armenia in 1828. Long and bitter resistance to Russian rule came from the Muslims of two regions—the Circassians, in the northwest, and the "mountaineers" of Daghestan, in the east. The Circassians were finally subdued in 1864, and the Imam Shamil, who led a holy war against the invader in Daghestan, surrendered in 1859. In 1864 the Caucasus was officially declared to be "pacified." For over half a century this land played for the Russians a role comparable with that of India's northwest frontier for the British. It proved a source of inspiration to some of the country's leading writers, among them Pushkin, Lermontov and Tolstoy, who described the wild beauty of its scenery, the customs of its peoples and the more colorful episodes of the conquest.

In the late nineteenth century the oil-rich Baku region became a major industrial center. The exploitation of these oil fields began in the early 1870's and owed much to Alfred Nobel, whose refinery *(overleaf)* was, in 1914, still the largest in the area. The completion in 1883 of the railway from Baku to Batum on the Black Sea, coupled with the construction in 1906 of a pipeline between these two towns, made it possible to sell the petroleum in the markets of the world. In 1913 the Baku oil fields produced over seven million tons of petroleum, four-fifths of Russia's output.

The Crimea is a region of geographical contrasts, and about three-quarters of it was, in this period, steppe land and an extension—across the narrow isthmus of Perekop—of the great Eurasian steppe. The Crimean Tatars (whose Khanate, based in Bakhchi Saray, was a successor-state of the Golden Horde) controlled this area until the Russian annexation of the peninsula by Catherine the Great in 1783. Farther south a range of limestone mountains falls steeply down onto a narrow fertile plain. The wine and the olive, brought to this coast by the Greek settlers of antiquity and cultivated in medieval times by the Byzantines and the Genoese, contrasted with the pastoral economy of the nomads beyond the mountains. In the nineteenth and early twentieth centuries members of the Russian imperial family and wealthy aristocrats, attracted by the Mediterranean climate of this southern coast, built palaces and villas overlooking the sea.

Preceding spread, 419. The fortress of Ananuri, to the north of Tiflis, commanding the Georgian military highway.

420A. The Grand Duke Michael, brother of Alexander II and viceroy of the Caucasus (1862–82), with his staff during a campaign in this region.

420B. Cossacks of the Russian army in the Caucasus.

The Nobel oil fields *(422, 423)*, and the "temple of the fire worshippers" *(421)* in Surakhani, near Baku, built in the thirteenth century. Azerbaijan, of which Baku is the main city, had for centuries been part of the Persian Empire.

424. Circassians.

426. Armenians from Erivan.

425. Gurians from western Georgia.

427. Khevsurs, a Georgian mountain tribe of the central Caucasus, c. 1890.

428. A princess of the Urusbiev tribe, in the Terek region.

429. A Kabardin married woman.

430. A Kabardin girl from the northwest Caucasus.

431. An Abkhaz woman from the Black Sea area, c. 1890.

432. A Georgian aristocrat from Tiflis.

433. Tiflis, on the banks of the Kura, became the capital of Iberia (eastern Georgia) in about the sixth century A.D. In the late nineteenth and early twentieth centuries it was the residence of the governor-general or viceroy of the Caucasus.

434. A Georgian inn.

435. Georgian aristocrats in Tiflis, c. 1865.

436. The Hotel de Londres in Erivan in 1900.

437–440. Armenian and gypsy musicians and dancers in Tiflis, c. 1865.

438. 439. 440.

441. An Armenian monk photographed by Count Nostitz in 1859.

442. Mtskheta, the ancient capital of Georgia and the original seat of the Georgian Catholicos-Patriarch. In the foreground is the Samtavro Monastery (c. 1200), and in the middle ground, the main Patriarchal Cathedral, built before 1010; the Jvari Church on the hill, dating from the sixth century, is the site where Saint Nino, who brought Christianity to Georgia, is said to have erected a cross in the fourth century.

443. The courtyard of an Armenian monastery. The church of Armenia, by declining to accept the canons of the Council of Chalcedon (A.D. 451), became monophysite in doctrine and has remained out of communion with the Orthodox Church.

444. The mountain village of Adish, south of the central Caucasus. As in other parts of the world, the towers were built to provide convenient vantage points for local fighting.

445. The village of Glola, in Ossetia, in the central Caucasus.

446. A funeral meal in Svaneti in the 1890's.

447. A valley in the central Caucasus, c. 1890.

448. The Georgian military highway crossed the central Caucasus range over the Darial Pass, linking Tiflis to Vladikavkaz and thus connecting central Georgia to European Russia.

448.

449–451. The palace at Bakhchi Saray, the residence of the Khans of the Crimea from the end of the fifteenth century until 1783.

452, 453. A vineyard in southern Crimea and oversize earthenware jars for storing wine.

454. A Tatar school in a Crimean village, c. 1888.

455. "Kennst du das Land, wo die Zitronen blühn?"

452.

453.

454.

456, 457. Odessa, founded by the Russians in 1794, owed much of its early development to Armand-Emmanuel, Duc de Richelieu, a French exile who became governor-general of New Russia and, after the Restoration, prime minister of France. During the nineteenth century Odessa, a cosmopolitan trading center with important Greek, Armenian and Jewish communities, became Russia's principal grain-exporting port. Its university, founded in 1865, was one of the chief centers of the 1905 Revolution.

458. Bringing grain from the countryside to Kiev. It was intended for export, via Odessa.

459. The synagogue in Odessa. The city's large Jewish community played an important role in its cultural life.

460. Jewish boys working in a tobacco factory in Feodosiya in the Crimea, c. 1898.

461. A Jewish family in Mozyr in White Russia.

462. A Jewish school in Romny in the Ukraine.

459.

460. 461. 462.

Папиросное Отдѣленіе

THE WESTERN
BORDERLANDS

64A.

64B.

THE WESTERN BORDERLANDS

SINCE THE MIDDLE AGES Russia's relations with her Western neighbors have been markedly ambiguous. On the one hand, the country's western borderlands seldom ceased to act as channels for trade, culture and diplomacy; and the majority of educated Russians, at least in recent times, have tended to regard their Western neighbors as fellow Europeans. On the other hand, since the thirteenth century the Russians have had to repel six major invasions from the West, two of which (in 1812 and 1941–42) came close to destroying their national existence. Hence it is hardly surprising that the need to secure the country's western borders has historically been a central preoccupation of Russian governments—a defensive stance that has often gone hand in hand with an active policy of expansion. One of its aims was to gain access to the Baltic Sea, a goal achieved in the early eighteenth century by Peter the Great.

Together with Estonia and Latvia, which were conquered in this period, four non-Russian areas lay within the western borders of the Russian Empire between 1855 and 1914: Bessarabia, Poland, Lithuania and Finland. Of all the subject peoples in the empire, the fiercely nationalistic Poles proved the hardest to assimilate. Between 1815 and 1830 Poland enjoyed the status of a constitutional kingdom within the empire, with the Russian emperor as king. However, two abortive Polish insurrections (1830–31 and 1863) increased the harshness of Russian rule, and the narrow-minded and chauvinistic policy of russification was

intensified after 1864. Finland, annexed in 1808, had for some ninety years a happier relationship with the imperial government: it had the status of a grand duchy united with Russia through the person of the monarch. The policy of russification, initiated in the last decade of the century, led to the assassination of the governor-general, N. I. Bobrikov, in 1904. The further growth of Finnish nationalism created a tense situation which was not to be resolved before the Revolution.

The annexation of part of the Ukraine in the seventeenth century, and especially the partitions of Poland in the late eighteenth, incorporated a large Jewish population into the Russian Empire. By 1900 the Jews numbered some three million, the great majority being compelled by law to live in the Pale of Settlement, which comprised the western and southwestern provinces. Discriminating measures against the Jews were alleviated during the reign of Alexander II, but became harsher in the anti-Semitic climate which prevailed during the last two reigns. The infamous pogroms became a recurrent feature from 1881 onwards, being particularly frequent and vicious in the 1880's and again between 1903 and 1906. They were not directly engineered by the imperial government, but were usually tolerated by the central and local officials. Exceptionally cruel was the decision to expel a large number of Jewish residents from Kiev (1886) and Moscow (1891).

Preceding spread, 463. Kamenets-Podolsky, on the river Smotrich (a tributary of the Dniester), close to the Austrian frontier. An important manufacturing and commercial center during the Middle Ages, the city was held successively—beginning in the twelfth century—by Russia, Lithuania, Poland and the Ottoman Empire, before reverting to Russia in 1793. The Polish fortress overlooks the town, c. 1885.

464A, 464B. Market scenes in western Russia.

Overleaf:
Kishinyov, the capital of Bessarabia, was the scene of a vicious pogrom in 1903, beginning on Easter Sunday, April 6. Spurred on by an anti-Semitic campaign in the local press, a mob terrorized the city for two days; hundreds of its 50,000 Jews were killed or injured, and over 700 houses and 600 business premises were destroyed. Not until the second day of rioting did the police and troops intervene. The Kishinyov massacre aroused a widespread outcry, both at home and abroad. But evidence suggests, as Leo Tolstoy indignantly charged, that the authorities had connived in the pogrom.

465, 467. Jewish families of Kishinyov.

466. Pogrom victims in a hospital.

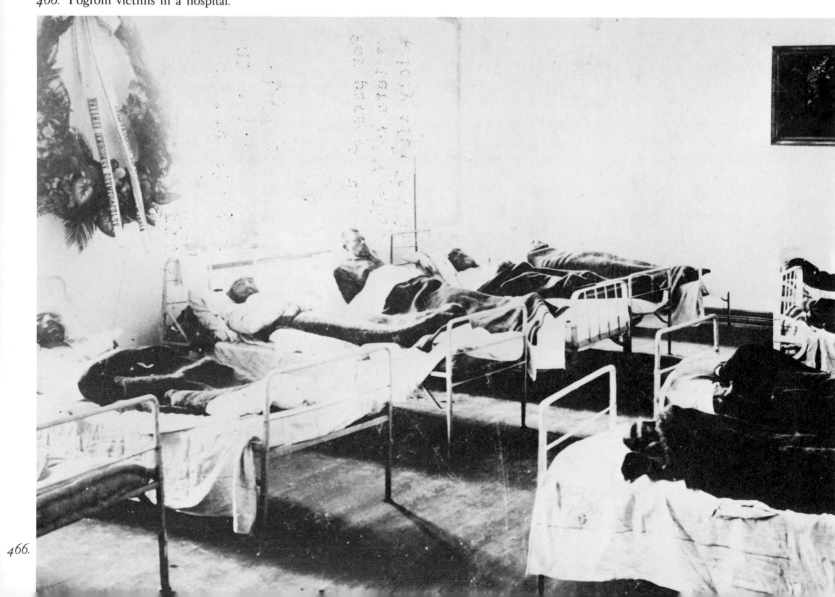

468. Mortally wounded victims.

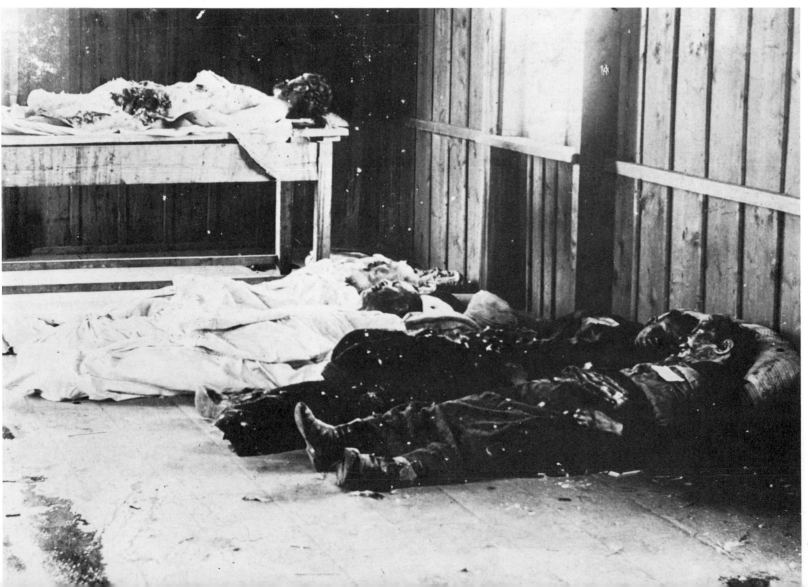

469–472. Galicia, on the northern slopes of the Carpathians, was the site of three major Russian offensives against the Austrian army during World War I (1914–15, 1916 and June 1917). The first two campaigns, remarkably successful at first, were turned into defeat by the inter-

vention of German forces; they did, however, contribute to Allied victory by relieving German pressure on the western front at two crucial moments: the battles of the Marne and Verdun.

473–476. The Russian front at Kalvariya: crossing the river
Sheshupe, north of Suvalki.

473·

474. 475. 476.

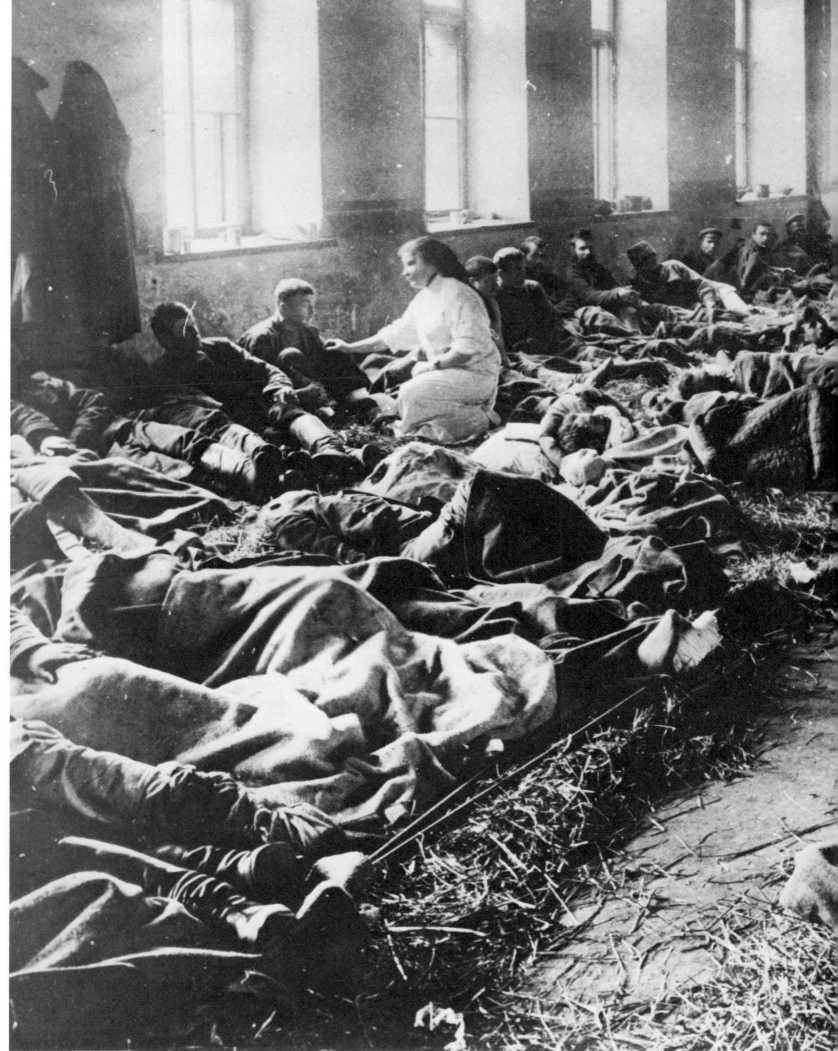

477. A Russian field hospital at Suvalki in Lithuania after a battle in February 1915.

PHOTOGRAPHIC CREDITS

The authors and publishers are grateful to the following for permission to reproduce photographs. Please note that the numbers refer to the photographs themselves rather than to page numbers, and that all unattributed photographs are courtesy of private collections (the names of those people who generously made their collections available are listed on page ix).

AUSTRIA

Museum für Völkerkunde, Vienna: 388, 390, 413, 414, 416, 418, 428–432.
Österreichische Nationalbibliothek, Vienna: 13.

DENMARK

The Royal Library, Copenhagen: 2, 9, 11, 92, 308, 312.

ENGLAND

Reproduced, by permission, from the Sir Benjamin Stone Collection of Photographs, Birmingham Reference Library: 252, 262, 268, 310.
Bodleian Library, Oxford: 285–291.
John Vere Brown, London: 420A, 420B, 435, 437–440.
Eastern Churches Association, London: 314, 316.
The Newcastle City Library: 368.
Radio Times Hulton Picture Library: 32.
Royal Anthropological Institute, London: B, D–H, L, O, Q.
Royal Archives, Windsor Castle, reproduced by gracious permission of Her Majesty the Queen: 7, 22.
The Royal Geographical Society, London: 325, 436, 444–447.
Royal Photographic Society of Great Britain: 6, 21, 23–25, 266, 309.
The Victoria and Albert Museum, London: 87.

FINLAND

Helsinki University Library: 82, 84, 271–273, 393.

National Museum of Finland: 54, 61, 63, 215, 218–221, 241, 255–258, 311, 313, 331–337, 349, 351–359, 372, 374, 375, 415, 417, 427, 453.
The Orthodox Church Museum, Kuopio: 83.

FRANCE

Agence France-Presse, Paris: 107.
Bibliothèque de l'Institut des Etudes Slaves, Paris: 152, 229, 230, 243–46.
Bibliothèque du Musée des Arts Décoratifs, Paris: 27–30, 33, 34, 254, 405, 409, 412, 424, 449–451.
Bibliothèque Nationale, Paris: 226, 227, 259.
Librairie de Sialsky, Paris: 104, 242, 302, 305–307.
Morskoye Sobraniye, Paris: 10.
Musée de l'Homme, Paris: T, 249, 317, 339B, 404, 454.
Roger-Viollet, Paris: 15–18, 20, 86, 102, 223, 303, 360, 361, 366, 367, 370, 371, 452, 458, 464B.
Société de Géographie Française, Paris: S, 97, 98, 100, 109, 217, 222, 225, 236, 237, 247, 269, 270, 282–284, 315, 319–323, 326, 327, 342, 345, 348, 350, 365, 381, 382, 384, 385, 387, 389, 391, 392, 400–403, 406–408, 410, 411, 419, 433, 434, 442, 457, 463.
Société Française de Photographie, Paris: 3, 64, 373, 441, 443.

GERMANY

Hamburgisches Museum für Völkerkunde: 324, 340, 341, 343, 344, 346, 376, 378, 383, 395–399.
Stadtgeschichtliche Sammlungen, Baden-Baden: 52.

Ullstein GMBH-Bilderdienst, Berlin: 14, 85, 88, 224, 260, 261, 362.

HOLLAND

International Institute of Social History: U–Y.

SWEDEN

The Royal Swedish Library, Stockholm: 110, 111, 304.

SWITZERLAND

Bernisches Historisches Museum: 330.
C.I.C.R., Archive Photographique, Geneva: 103, 477.
Musée de l'Elysée, Lausanne: 112, 274, 292, 329.

UNITED STATES

Courtesy of American Museum of Natural History, New York: 338, 339A, 364, 377, 379, 380, 386.
Bakhmetev Archive, Rare Book and Manuscript Library, Columbia University, New York: 69–71, 180, 248.
Hoover Institution, Stanford, California: 275–281.
Library of Congress, Washington, D.C.: 101, 347, 363, 369, 456.
Sam Wagstaff, New York: 250.
Daniel Wolf Collection, New York: 464A.
Courtesy of YIVO Institute for Jewish Research, New York: 394, 459–462, 465–468.

We are also indebted to Dr. Martin Gilbert, whose *Russian History Atlas* (Macmillan, 1972) was most helpful in the preparation of the map on pages xii–xiii.

ABOUT THE AUTHORS

CHLOE OBOLENSKY was born in Athens in 1942. Educated in England and France, she studied scenic design in Paris and began her distinguished career in the theater as Lila de Nobili's assistant. She has designed sets and costumes for productions at La Scala and the Comédie Française, as well as for French television, and has worked with Gian Carlo Menotti and Franco Zeffirelli on various projects.

MAX HAYWARD was a Fellow of St. Antony's College at Oxford University and a specialist in the Soviet period of Russian literature. He translated many important Russian works, including Pasternak's *Doctor Zhivago* (with the late Manya Harari), Mandelstam's *Hope Against Hope* and *Hope Abandoned* and, most recently, Olga Ivinskaya's *Captive of Time*. He also translated poetry by Mayakovski, Yetushenko, Voznesneski and Akhmatova. He died in 1979. As Leonard Schapiro has written, "The death of Max Hayward at the early age of fifty-four has deprived us of one of the few outstanding scholars in the Russian field who have emerged in Britain since the end of the war. The combination of brilliant linguistic talent, an elegant style and scrupulous standards of scholarship made him into one of the finest translators from the Russian of all time. As an editor, lecturer and essayist he interpreted for the English reader what was best in modern Russian culture (which in Soviet terms means mainly works which the authorities reject) with sympathy, original insight and incisive understanding. The essay in this volume illustrates the depth of his knowledge of the culture of the past on which his interpretation of more recent works was based."